I0414023

Editor-in-Chief and Founder:
   Lyndon H. LaRouche, Jr.
Editorial Board: *Lyndon H. LaRouche, Jr. , Helga Zepp-LaRouche, Robert Ingraham, Tony Papert, Gerald Rose, Dennis Small, Jeffrey Steinberg, William Wertz*
Co-Editors: *Robert Ingraham, Tony Papert*
Managing Editor: *Nancy Spannaus*
Technology: *Marsha Freeman*
Books: *Katherine Notley*
Ebooks: *Richard Burden*
Graphics: *Alan Yue*
Photos: *Stuart Lewis*
Circulation Manager: *Stanley Ezrol*

INTELLIGENCE DIRECTORS
Counterintelligence: *Jeffrey Steinberg, Michele Steinberg*
Economics: *John Hoefle, Marcia Merry Baker, Paul Gallagher*
History: *Anton Chaitkin*
Ibero-America: *Dennis Small*
Russia and Eastern Europe: *Rachel Douglas*
United States: *Debra Freeman*

INTERNATIONAL BUREAUS
Bogotá: *Miriam Redondo*
Berlin: *Rainer Apel*
Copenhagen: *Tom Gillesberg*
Houston: *Harley Schlanger*
Lima: *Sara Madueño*
Melbourne: *Robert Barwick*
Mexico City: *Gerardo Castilleja Chávez*
New Delhi: *Ramtanu Maitra*
Paris: *Christine Bierre*
Stockholm: *Ulf Sandmark*
United Nations, N.Y.C.: *Leni Rubinstein*
Washington, D.C.: *William Jones*
Wiesbaden: *Göran Haglund*

ON THE WEB
e-mail: eirns@larouchepub.com
www.larouchepub.com
www.executiveintelligencereview.com
www.larouchepub.com/eiw
Webmaster: *John Sigerson*
Assistant Webmaster: *George Hollis*
Editor, Arabic-language edition: *Hussein Askary*

EIR (ISSN 0273-6314) *is published weekly (50 issues), by EIR News Service, Inc., P.O. Box 17390, Washington, D.C. 20041-0390. (703) 297-8434*

European Headquarters: E.I.R. GmbH, Postfach Bahnstrasse 9a, D-65205, Wiesbaden, Germany
Tel: 49-611-73650
Homepage: http://www.eir.de
e-mail: info@eir.de
Director: Georg Neudecker

Montreal, Canada: 514-461-1557
eir@eircanada.ca

Denmark: EIR - Danmark, Sankt Knuds Vej 11, basement left, DK-1903 Frederiksberg, Denmark.
Tel.: +45 35 43 60 40, Fax: +45 35 43 87 57. e-mail: eirdk@hotmail.com.

Mexico City: EIR, Sor Juana Inés de la Cruz 242-2 Col. Agricultura C.P. 11360 Delegación M. Hidalgo, México D.F.
Tel. (5525) 5318-2301
eirmexico@gmail.com

Canada Post Publication Sales Agreement #40683579

Postmaster: Send all address changes to *EIR*, P.O. Box 17390, Washington, D.C. 20041-0390.

Signed articles in *EIR* represent the views of the authors, and not necessarily those of the Editorial Board.

Our Next 40 Years' Partnership with Russia, China and India

EIR Contents

www.larouchepub.com Volume 44, Number 26, June 30, 2017

*Cover
This Week*

*Northern polar
view of the Earth.*

NASA

OUR NEXT 40 YEARS' PARTNERSHIP WITH RUSSIA, CHINA AND INDIA

I. Lyndon LaRouche's 'Manhattan Project'

Beautiful City

Όμορφη πόλη

by Dean Andromidas

FIRST OF THREE PARTS

June 24—In February 2017, I was struck by the discussion in a meeting of Lyndon and Helga Zepp-LaRouche with some of their associates, where the question of a beautiful city came up during a discussion of voice placement. The issue was raised in the context of building new cities in the United States, which should have an important element of beauty imbued in them. The discussion provoked me to give some thought, and some work to it, and to present some rough ideas.

To explore the idea of the Beautiful City, let us look at two examples: Athens and Manhattan.

I say Athens and not just "ancient" Athens, because the city has had an uninterrupted life of over three thousand years. It is, not was, the city of immortal Plato and the poets, and has continued to produce philosophers and poets through the centuries, to this very day. It has never ceased in its role as light-bearer of universal civilization and the struggle for true freedom, whether against the Persian or British empires or the chains of a false ideology.

It was in the dark days of 1941, when the eternal city was under the brutal occupation of the Nazis, that a 16-year-old youth, upon hearing that the brave people of beautiful Crete were still fiercely resisting the Nazi invasion of their island, knew at once that he could not stand idle. In the dark of night, he and a comrade

creative commons/Christophe Meneboeuf

The Acropolis in Athens, Greece.

launched a flanking operation. They secretly climbed the Acropolis and removed the Nazi flag, replacing it with the blue and white Greek flag. This act is credited as the first act of resistance in Nazi-occupied Europe. In 2001, that same youth, Manolis Glezos, now over 90 years of age—with another resistance fighter, the great modern composer Mikis Theodorakis—launched another resistance movement against the financial oligarchy which has been looting and destroying their country and their city.

Courtesy of Mikis Theodorakis

Mikis Theodorakis

The Greeks of today speak in principle the same language as Plato and they love their city just as deeply as the great philosophers and poets. In this time of terrible crisis for Greeks of today, looking upon the Acropolis, crowned by the most famous of edifices, the Parthenon, gives them the strength to resist, knowing that their city has made some of the most important contributions to universal culture. It is this Athens that bears the crucial attributes of a "beautiful city."

Athens embodies the Hellenic conception of "polis," which, rather than being exclusive, is inclusive not just of its "native" citizens but foreigners as well, according to the Greek concept that sees the stranger as a guest who might indeed have something to offer the city, especially in the way of ideas. One sees this in perhaps less poetic terms, but in the spirit of its times, in New York City.

At the center of this Athens is the Acropolis, for many centuries the religious and civic center of the city, and now still, as it has always been, its spiritual center. Surrounding it was the Agora or marketplace, from which a road and long walls linked the city to the port of Piraeus and the *demes* or city districts. This is much like every city, ancient, renaissance or modern. There are many professional city planners capable of designing the functionality of a city in which most people would be satisfied living and working. So these attributes I leave to the professional.

But let's look at the Acropolis and its crown jewel, the Parthenon, which lies at the very heart of the city, if not the very heart of Greece and Western Civilization. Everyone knows the history: Initiated by Pericles following the victory over the Persians, and designed by the architects Iktinos and Kallikrates and the sculptor Pheidias, this was the most amazing of buildings in the history of civilized man. No other building shares all the attributes of this temple. Although there is one that endeavors to, which I will discuss later.

I will not attempt a detailed analysis of the Parthenon, I leave that to the experts. Nonetheless a comment on its most celebrated feature, its curvature, is important for my purpose. As is known, there is not one straight line in the entire edifice. No two parts are identical. It has been suggested for centuries now, that the purpose of this curvature is to correct the distortion imparted onto straight lines by the eye of the viewer. Panos Valavanis, one of the archeologists involved in the restoration project of the Parthenon, now in its third decade, wrote:

The Agora or market place surrounding the Acropolis.

The Parthenon in Athens.

creative commons/Steve Swayne

"It is improbable that this entire nexus of features, invisible on first glance, was of the nature of visual adjustments or a way of neutralizing optical illusion, as had been assumed from late Antiquity. It is actually a recondite mesh enclosing the entire building, even its least accessible parts, and was created deliberately in order to serve purely aesthetic aims. It was intended to insufflate the pulse of life and movement into the monument, to unfetter it from static rigidity, imparting a covert harmony, which, according to Heraclitus, was more important than the overt... Because we cannot accept that they were applied only to satisfy the needs of the monument's creators. Everything must also have served the aesthetic demands of an entire society, to which, in the last analysis, the monument was addressed."

There is no mystery here. Up until the liberation of Athens in 1833, western Europeans could not easily examine the Greek monuments. Architecture was dominated by Roman classicism, as very misleadingly interpreted by the Roman engineer Vitruvius and his ten easy lessons on architecture. Once Athens was liberated, German and French architects, artists and poets began visiting the city. King Otto, the first modern king of Greece, moved to preserve the Acropolis as an archaeological site, bringing professional architects and archaeologists to prepare the site and begin a close examination. It was observed that the curvature was not derived from arcs of circles, but derived from conic sec-

tions, including parabolic curves. This conical curvature contrasts with the circular curvature of Roman architecture.

This curvature in conic sections applied to all the elements of the building, including the columns, stylobate, the entablature, the pediment, and so on. There were no straight lines and no plumb surfaces.

By contrast to the circular, the conical and parabolic cast soft shadows, and in combination with the highly polished marble positively affect the *chiaroscuro* of the building. This generation of light and shadow not only generated the sense of depth, but contributes to an overall sense of metaphorical ambiguity central to any form of art, whether literary, plastic or musical. This point is very important in relation to the painted parts of the Parthenon, which are poorly understood.

Charles Blanc, one of the first to closely analyze the Parthenon in his *Grammaire des Arts du Dessin*, wrote that the Parthenon had the character of the Sublime, and observing it "is like the sudden encounter with infinity," for "unlike beauty, which is man's domain," the sublime places the observer "above and beyond us."

King Otto's chief architect, Joseph Hoffer, wrote: "The system of curved lines" which exhibited a "perfect logic," had enabled Greek architects "to infuse the lifeless forms of art with a breath of living Nature, for Nature avoids the rectilinear and develops its most attractive forms in swelling curves."

Hoffer's contemporary, Charles Schnaase, wrote in his *Geschichte der bildenden Künste* "a feeling of life," conveyed by this curvature, "inspired the whole building, dispelling its mathematical rigidity."

The English astronomer J. Norman Lockyer observed that the Parthenon is an Egyptian Temple made beautiful. Lockyer wrote: What would the Greeks do, who were the first Europeans to be exposed to Egyptian ideas, and after observing Egypt's "massive and glorious" temples, and "fired with Greek ideals of the beautiful, determined that their new land should not remain altarless?"

What would they do? They would naturally

adapt the Egyptian temple to the new surroundings, climatic among others. The open courts and flat roofs of Egyptian temples would give way to covered courts and sloping roofs to deal with a more copious rainfall: and it is curious to note that the chief architectural differences have this simple origin. The small financial resources of a colony would be reason good enough for a *cella* not far from the entrance, with courts surrounding it under the now necessary roof. The intuitive love of beauty would do the rest, and make it a *sine qua non* that the rosy-fingered dawn would be observable, and that the colored light of the rising sun in the more boreal clime should render glorious a state statue of the divinity.

creative commons

Nikos Kazantzakis

Oriented to the Pleiades

In the case of the Parthenon, and following the Egyptian model, the temple was orientated to the Pleiades constellation in such a way that the priests could observe it, so as to foretell the rising of the sun at various feast days, thereby giving the priests the time to prepare for the ceremony. (For a full discussion of the Parthenon's orientation see: *The Dawn of Astronomy; A Study of the Temple-Worship and Mythology of the Ancient Egyptians*, by J. Norman Lockyer, pp. 413-424.)

Greece's most accomplished and beloved literary figure of the 20th century, Nikos Kazantzakis, wrote late in his life, "This temple is a mystery to me. I can never see it the same way twice; it seems to change constantly, come to life, undulate while remaining motionless, play games with light and the human eye."

Nonetheless as a young rebellious youth he at first rejected it, writing:

"I felt that the Parthenon was an even number such as two or four. Even numbers run contrary to my heart; I want nothing to do with them, their lives are too comfortably arranged, they stand on their feet much to solidly and have not the slightest desire to change position. They are satisfied, conservative, without anxieties; they have solved every problem, translated every desire into reality, and grown calm. It was the odd number which conforms to the rhythm of my heart. The life of the odd number is not at all comfortably arranged. The odd number does not like this world the way it finds it, but seeks to change it, add to it, push it further. It stands on one foot, holds the other ready in the air, and wants to depart. Where to? To the following even number, in order to halt for an instant, catch its breath, and work up fresh momentum."

Nonetheless with each successive visit he soon discovered that the Parthenon was an odd number:

But after each new return from Attica's olive groves and the Saronic Gulf, the hidden harmony, casting aside its veils one by one, slowly, gradually revealed itself to my mind. Each time I climbed the Acropolis again, the Parthenon seemed to be swaying slightly, as in a motionless dance— swaying and breathing…

This initiation lasted for months, perhaps years. I do not remember the exact day when I stood completely initiated before the Parthenon and my heart bounded like a young calf. This temple that towered before me, what a trophy it was, what a collaboration between mind and heart, what a supreme fruit of human effort! Space had been conquered; distinctions between small and large had vanished. Infinity entered this narrow, magical parallelogram carved out by man, entered leisurely and took its repose there. Time had been conquered as well; the lofty moment had been transformed into eternity.

I allowed my gaze to creep over the warm, sun-nourished marble. It touched the stones and rummaged through them like a hand, uncovering the hidden mysteries; it clung to them and refused to depart. I saw the seemingly parallel columns imperceptibly incline their capitals one toward the other so that concertedly, with tenderness and strength, they might sustain the sacred pediments entrusted to them.

Never have undulations created lines so irreproachably straight. Never have numbers and music coupled with such understanding, such love.

Kazantsakis often wrote that the true mission of mankind is to "turn matter into spirit," and indeed the Parthenon is a celebrated example of that principle. (*Report to Greco*, Nikos Kazantzakis, pp. 136—138.)

The American Hudson River School painter, Frederic Edwin Church, spent several weeks in Athens in 1869, studying the Greek ruins, and wrote to his friend Nicholas Biddle Kittell:

Artist Frederic Edwin Church

The Parthenon

The Parthenon is certainly the culmination of the genius of man in architecture. Every column, every ornament, every molding asserts the superiority which is claimed for even the shattered remains of the once proud temple over all other buildings by man.

I have made architectural drawings of the Parthenon and fancied before I came to Athens that I had a good idea of its merits. But in reality I knew it not. Daily I study its stones and feel its inexpressible charm of beauty growing upon my senses. I am glad I came here—and shall try and secure as much material as possible. I think a great picture could be made of the ruins. They are very picturesque as well as imposing and the color is superb.

Again in a letter to William H. Osborn, he wrote, "I recently visited Greece—Athens—I was delighted. The Parthenon is a wonderful work of the human intellect. No photograph can convey even a faint impression of its majesty and beauty... fragments of sculpture are strewn all about—and let me say that I think Athens is the place for sculpture—to be sure in Rome they have famous things—mostly brought from Greece, but on the classic ground itself everything is in its place. The Greeks had noble conceptions. They gave a large god-

like air to all they did and the fragments and bits are full of merit. I spent over two weeks there with immense pleasure and profit... and when I returned—Rome with its gross architecture looked cheap and vulgar. "

Church made his painting of the Parthenon: it can be seen hanging in the Metropolitan Museum of art.

Let's have a look at the "sacred pediments" entrusted to this temple of temples. These are formed by sculptures arranged in three categories. There are the pediments, the second are the metopes, which are set on the entablature above the columns, and the third is the frieze on the wall.

Those on the pediments celebrate the deity of the city, Athena—first her birth, on the east pediment, and her conflict with Poseidon on the west. While all the principal gods are there, the Parthenon is a celebration of Athena, the patron god of Athens and, most importantly, the god of knowledge, marking her as the goddess for all humanity. Indeed, she has been transformed from a patron god of the city to a principle upon which the city, if not all of Greece, rests.

The metopes depict, in snapshot form, the mythological battles—first the Gigantomachy, the battle between the Gods and their challengers, the Titans. Next is the Amazonomachy, the battle between the Amazons and the Greeks, in which the Athenian hero Theseus plays a crucial part. This is followed by the scenes of the sack of Troy with emphasis on Demophon and Akamas, the sons of Theseus who took part in it. Lastly

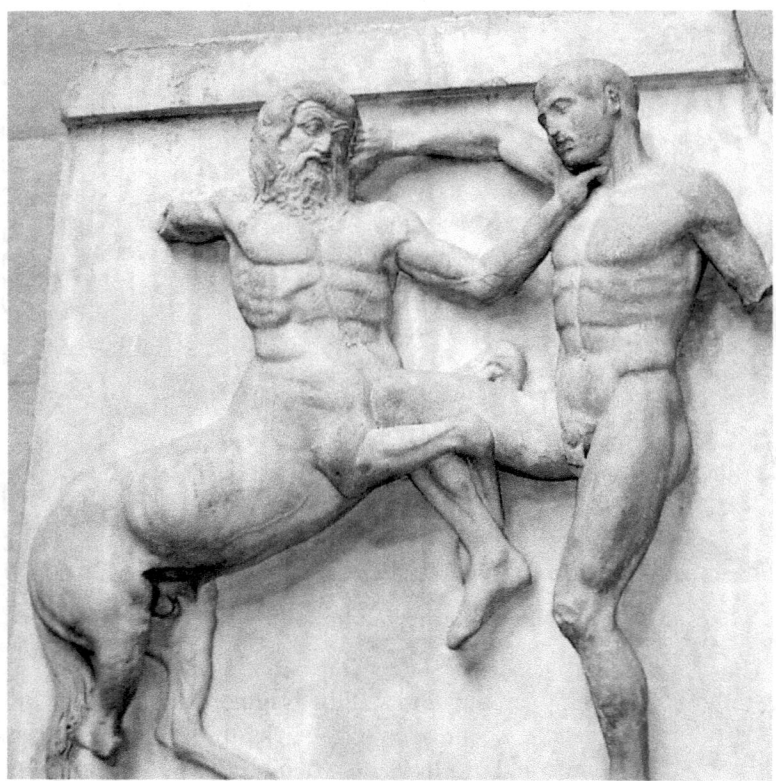

Parthenon Metope: Centaur and Lapith in combat.

creative commons

their works in the Dionysos theater on the slope at the base of the Acropolis' south wall below the Parthenon, serving as the counterpoint between the "Frozen Music of Architecture," as Goethe once described Architecture, and the music of the poet.

Then on the other side of the Acropolis is the Agora, or market place. It is here where one found Socrates holding his immortal dialogues, transforming art into what we call "philosophy."

While volumes can be written on the beautiful city of Athens, it is the Acropolis and its Parthenon that captures its essence and embody all the principles we need to know.

In fear of belaboring the reader with yet another long quote from our modern Greek poet, I must nonetheless quote below another passage from Kazantzakis' *Report to Greco*, describing the conclusion of a tour through Greece he made after graduating from university—which would be about 1905, although he wrote this shortly before his death in 1956. So it was as an older man reflecting on his own development.

there is the Centauromachy, the battle between the Thessalian tribe of the Lapiths and the Centaurs, half man-half horse. The defeat of the latter was secured through the decisive intervention of Theseus.

The third category of sculpture is the frieze relief displayed behind the outer colonnade. This is perhaps the most masterful of all. It is the procession of the Panathenaia, a celebration held every four years in honor of the Goddess, where the entire city as well as delegations from all of Greece participate. Archaeological evidence is said to suggest that this was not in the original plan but was the result of a political decision. No other Greek temple displayed a relief at this location. Like the temple itself, it is a relief in motion.

So here on this one temple can be seen Gods of the Hellenistic world, its mythologies and its citizens. There has been much commentary on the symbolism and relationships of these three sets of sculpture, some saying they depict the conflict between Man and the Gods, Civilized man, the Greeks and the Barbarians, etc. But who are we to make such commentaries? The most truthful commentaries on these relationships were by the Greek tragic poets themselves, who performed

When a Greek travels through Greece, his journey becomes converted in this fatal way into a laborious search to find his duty. How is he to become worthy of our ancestors? How can he continue his national tradition without disgracing it? A severe unsilenceable responsibility weighs heavily on his shoulders, on the shoulders of every living Greek. The name itself possesses an invincible, magical force. Every person born in Greece has the duty to continue the eternal Greek legend.

In the modern Greek, no region of his homeland calls forth a disinterested quiver of aesthetic appreciation. The region has a name; it is Marathon, Salamis, Olympia, Thermopylae, Mistra, and it is bound up with a memory: here we were disgraced, there we won glory. All at once the region is transformed into much-wept, wide-roving history, and the Greek pilgrim's entire soul is thrown into turmoil. Each Greek region is so soaked with successes and failures possessing world-wide echoes, so filled with human struggle, that it is elevated into an austere lesson which we cannot escape. It becomes a cry, and our duty is to hear this cry.

Greece's position is truly tragic; on the shoulders of every modern Greek it places a duty at once dangerous and extremely difficult to carry out. We bear an extremely heavy responsibility. New forces are rising from the East, new forces are rising from the West, and Greece, caught as always between the two colliding impulses once more becomes a whirlpool. Following the tradition of reason and empirical inquiry, the West bounds forward to conquer the world; the East, prodded by frightening subconscious forces, likewise darts forward to conquer the world. Greece is placed in the middle; it is the world's geographical and spiritual crossroads. Once again its duty is to reconcile these two monstrous impulses by finding a synthesis. Will it succeed?

It is a sacred and most bitter fate. At the end of my trip though Greece I was filled with tragic, unexpected questions. Starting with beauty, we had arrived at the agonies of our times and the present-day duty imposed on every Greek. Today, a man who is alive—who thinks, loves, and struggles—is no longer able to amble in a carefree way, to appreciate beauty. The struggle today is spreading like a conflagration, and no fire brigade can insure our safety. Every man is struggling and burning along with all humanity. And the Greek nation is struggling more than all the rest. This is its fate.

The circle closed. My eyes filled with Greece. It seems to me that my mind ripened in those three months. What were the most precious spoils of this intellectual campaign? I believe they were these: I saw more clearly the historic mission of Greece, placed as it is between East and West; I realized that her supreme achievement is not beauty but the struggle for liberty. I felt Greece's tragic destiny more deeply, and also what a heavy duty is imposed on every Greek.

I believe that immediately following my pilgrimage through Greece, I was ripe enough to begin the years of maturity. It was not beauty which led the way and ushered me to manhood, it was responsibility.

If I had summarized this passage in two sen-

tences, would I have so beautifully expressed an idea that holds true today as it did a half century ago when these words were written?

The question immediately arises—can walking the streets of Manhattan evoke similar feelings, similar commitments, similar responsibilities?

Manhattan as the Beautiful City

Can we learn something of the beautiful city, Manhattan, from Arthur Miller's *Death of a Salesman*? Does that play, separated from us by one or two generations, bear comparison to immortal works of the Greek poets? Could someone so profane as to marry Marilyn Monroe bear comparison to the tragic poets? Yet with a closer look at the play, one will soon discover that nothing could be more at the very heart of New York society than this play.

The image of the "salesman," forever in my mind, whom I saw every day in the 1970s on Seventh Avenue; the well dressed, sassy-looking men rolling their wheeled sample cases, hailing cabs in their thick New York accents. Selling the wares of the famous, or infamous, in the "fashion" center of the world, a world with its own internal hierarchy, at the bottom of which were the seamstresses and delivery boys, up to the aristocratic layers that began with the "cutter" and ended

Library of Congress

Men pulling racks of clothing on a sidewalk in the New York Garment District in 1955.

with the boss, who in this most New York of industries could in one season become a millionaire, and in the next a bankrupt. The salesman found himself somewhere in between the skilled cutter, protected by his union, and the boss whose fortunes were inseparable from his own success or failure.

It was also the heart of the Jewish community of New York, the world's largest outside of Israel. But these Jews did not come from Palestine, they came from Central and Eastern Europe and the Russian Empire, having arrived in New York in the first decades of the 20th century, fleeing pogroms, persecution and poverty. They brought with them the progressive and socialist ideas of their time, as well as a high degree of culture and the arts, enriching every aspect of the city.

Arthur Miller came out of this environment. His parents were Austrian Jews. Miller was born on the upper West Side of Manhattan when his father, the proprietor of a garment factory with 400 employees, was rich—only to lose everything when the "crash" came. Miller soon found himself moving to Brooklyn: He had to work to pay his way through school. As he said in an interview, salesmen were very much part of his family experience. He too was a man of the left, a "progressive."

In fact, this play, clearly the best play Miller wrote, and arguably the only good play he wrote, was not written by him. It was written and inspired by the muses of Manhattan. Indeed, in an interview given a few years before his death, he insisted that he had not written it. "I was the stenographer. I could hear the characters. I could hear them literally," as he took down the words of the characters speaking in the silence of his mind in clear and powerful words.

In an interview many years after he wrote the play, Miller recounted that Willy Loman, as is often the case, was modeled on a real person he had known, whose life represented "failure in the face of surrounding success. He was the ultimate climber up the ladder who was,

Eileen Darby/Keystone Features/Fair use

Lee J. Cobb, seated, with Arthur Kennedy, left, and Cameron Mitchell in the 1949 production of Death of a Salesman.

constantly, being stepped on. His fingers were being stepped on by those climbing past him. My empathy for him was immense. And I mean, how could he possibly have succeeded? There was no way… He committed suicide… The play was basically looking from the edge of the grave at life."

In an interview in 1949, on the eve of the play's opening, Miller told the *New York Times* that Loman, as does every man, "has an image of himself which fails in one way or another to correspond with reality. It's the discrepancy between illusion and reality that matters. The closer a man gets to knowing himself, the less likely he is to trip up on his own illusions." The play poignantly reveals how Loman's self-delusion is transmitted to his sons, who are seen as unable to deal with reality.

He said that he knew the play was good when he finished it, but did not understand its impact until his publicist came to read the manuscript and was brought to uncontrolled tears. In fact, at the play's debut, when the final curtain came down, there was nothing but silence in the theater, for the entire audience had been reduced to tears.

Bernard Gimbel, the owner of the famous Gimbel's department stores was in that tear-filled audience, and is said to have given orders the next day that no employee should ever be dismissed for being overaged.

As a prologue to this story: Three of the most important creators of that first performance, Lee J. Cobb (born Leo Jacobi), who played Willy Loman, the director, Elia Kazan, and Arthur Miller himself were all forced to appear before the House Un-American Activities Committee because of their alleged communist sympathies. The first two named names. Miller did not.

Beautiful city? one protests, that drives a hapless man to suicide? Yet I am reminded of the lines of Alcinous, in Homer's *Odyssey*, who upon seeing Odysseus weeping while the minstrel sings the *Iliad*, says,

...Why to heare
The Fate of Greece and Ilion
   mourne you so?
The Gods have done it; as to all
   they do
Destine to destruction, that
   from thence may rise
A Poeme to instruct posterities.

Sacred Soil

Miller's play expressed a universal truth that could move audiences throughout the United States as well as the world. It was translated into Greek and performed in Athens in 1949 with incidental music written by the equally beloved 20th Century Greek composer Manos Hadjidakis. But this play could not have been written in any other city than New York. Willy Loman's imaginary home is in the Flatbush section of Brooklyn, where Miller grew up. Loman was employed by a company in Manhattan's West Side garment district. One of his sons is obviously a buyer for Macy's or Gimbel's department store. Loman held a 25-year mortgage with which he bought his house when it was almost a suburb of Manhattan, but it is now suffocated by the surrounding apartment houses which push up against the windows, blocking out the light and air. This is New York, a city that undergoes dramatic change over the course from one generation to another.

When the first subway was built in the three thousand year-old Athens, the ancient city was exposed like the deep roots of an old oak tree, exposing what seemed another strange world, yet it was every bit Athens just as much as its 19th Century Parliament and the Athens Hilton.

While Athens is over thirty centuries old, New York is a mere four, and has not yet passed two and a half centuries as the greatest city of the independent Republic of the United States. Yet like Athens, the millions of tons of asphalt, concrete, brick and mortar cover, as the poets would say, a "sacred blood-soaked soil" where trod the men and women who struggled, fought and died for the same principle as did the Athenians—that is freedom and necessity.

creative commons/Ben Crowe
Socrates

Living under the shadow of the Parthenon, the modern Athenian is confronted every day with this struggle for that ancient principle, freedom and necessity. Set high on the Acropolis, the Parthenon can be seen from every part of the city, even from neighboring islands. If one is blind, one can always touch it with the conceit that Pericles, Socrates or Plato also touched it at that very spot.

While much of Athens is a post-World War II city, walking through it one is not only confronted with the great Acropolis and Agora which lie at its very center, but as one walks through it, one comes upon open archaeological sites where the ancient city, including the Greek, Hellenistic and Roman periods, reminds the viewer that below the tons of concrete and asphalt, he is walking on sacred soil. One is often confronted with an ancient church and chapel, confronting the viewer with the Early Christian Byzantine. Walking through the Plaka, or the old city below the Acropolis, one can see buildings from the period of Ottoman occupation and early independence. Further into the city can be seen the grand neoclassical buildings of early independence, the Parliament, the Law University and others.

The ability to see, and even touch one's history across its entirety cannot help but have a powerful impact on each successive generation, and is one of the crucial elements of the beautiful city.

While New York is famous for its towering skyscrapers, it has no acropolis capped by a Parthenon. But if one looks for it, one can find sacred, blood-soaked soil, uncovered and exposed where the eyes can see, the feet can tread and the fingers can touch.

Athens has its Marathon and Salamis where the defeat of an Empire assured the posterity of Hellenism for eternity. The first battle for an independent United States was the battle for New York, which began within hours of the signing of the Declaration of Independence. While not our Marathon or Salamis, it exposed the weakness of an Empire. Perhaps it was our Thermopylae. Though ending in defeat, that battle, against overwhelming odds, lasted more than four months, and the British failure to capture or destroy Washington's army served the strategic goal of demonstrating to the King and his army that they would have to fight for every inch of territory.

A review of that battle will serve the purpose of this report, which is to link culture and history with the topography of the living beautiful city, as it is a battle that was fought throughout almost the entire area of today's New York City. While most of the battlefield is covered with concrete, asphalt and bricks, small patches of the original battlefield still push up through the modern megalopolis. They are marked by monuments that have almost been forgotten in the everyday hustle and bustle of the city.

painting by C.W. Peale
Nathanael Greene

Washington's strategy rested on the principles upon which we sought to create a nation. These principles are well expressed by one of Washington's generals, Nathanael Greene, a native of Rhode Island. He died soon after the revolution and his story is not well known. He held fast to those principles and fought across the territory of what would become the great nation for which he was fighting, not to defend it, for it did not yet exist, but to create it.

In January of 1776, it was still being debated whether the colonies would remain a party of discontents demanding relief from the injustices of the "mother country," or declare independence with the purpose of creating a new nation that would give territory to their principles, that would stand on the surface of this planet, and that could be called a "nation." Greene, writing—on the eve of the departure to New York of Washington's army from Boston, which it had recently occupied—to his friend and mentor, Governor Ward, who represented Rhode Island at the Continental Congress, encouraged him to support the proclamation of independence:

Heaven has decreed that tottering empire to ir-

retrievable ruin; and, thanks to God, since Providence has so determined it, America must raise an empire of permanent duration, supported upon the grand pillars of truth, freedom, and religion, based upon justice, and defended by her own patriotic sons. Permit me then to recommend from the sincerity of my heart, ready at all times to bleed in my country's cause, a declaration of independence; and call upon the world and the great God who governs it, to witness the necessity, propriety, and rectitude thereof. My worthy friend, the interests of mankind hang upon that truly worthy body of which you are a member. You stand the representative not of America only, but of the whole world, the friends of liberty, and the supporters of the rights of human nature. How will posterity, millions yet unborn, bless the memory of those brave patriots who are now hastening the consummation of freedom, truth and religion." (*General Greene*, by Francis Vinton Greene, pages 31-32. Kennikat Press, Port Washington, NY./London.)

Thus Washington's strategic conception was first to demonstrate to the British that the they were fighting not against a nation or a country, but a principle, and a principle has no topography that can be seen and tread upon. It cannot be crushed by cannon-shot or invaded and conquered by a well-armed and trained army. It is weightless and has no surface. It is an idea held in the breast and soul of a man and woman. You may kill that man or woman, but you will never destroy that principle.

Nonetheless Washington had to submit this strategic principle to the demands of the topography of the battlefield.

Washington knew his adversary well. The British commander, General William Howe, was well-known to Washington from the French and Indian War. While he was well-trained in the art of warfare, that art was of the set-piece warfare characteristic of the warring monarchs of Europe, where victory and the end of the war could be won through destroying the adversary's army in one great battle. With a poorly-trained army supplied on a shoestring budget, Washington would not fight that type of war. His army would be everywhere, yet nowhere at the same time. He might lose a battle, but his army would withdraw from the field intact to fight yet another day. But at the end of a long seven years, it would be the British, at Yorktown, who would lose an entire army.

This was a strategy that would drive the British commanders mad. They were also fighting under severe limitations. While Britain had a huge fleet that commanded the seas, their army, while well-trained, was severely limited in numbers, and had to be supplemented with expensive Hessian mercenaries. With their long supply lines stretching all the way to Europe, they had to carefully husband both their manpower and supplies. For example, the Americans would deny the British horses, forcing them to ship horses all the way from Europe, thus the continentals had a greater cavalry then the British.

The Battlefield of New York City

New York City of 1776 was like a miniature England. In fact it was considered the most English of the English colonies. Being the capital of the colony of New York, its governor was the embodiment of the British Sovereign. Like the king whom he represented, he had a twelve-man executive council through which he made all important decisions on running the colony and city. There was also a colonial assembly, and as in Westminster it had its loyalists and opposition, all in order to have heated debates—but like those of the debating societies of Oxford or Cambridge, their debates were of little consequence, because all important decisions were made by the sovereign's representative. Then there was the City Council, modeled after those

Oil on canvas by William Walcutt.

Pulling down the statue of King George III in New York City in 1776.

of England, that is to say impotent by design.

This little London also had its own aristocracy, with their town-houses in the city, which then only covered the lower tip of Manhattan, but also landed estates, in upper Manhattan and what are now Brooklyn, Queens, the Bronx and Westchester. Visitors from the "mother country" always felt at home in what for Englishmen was a congenial environment.

Yet in this most English of Colonial cities, filled with loyalists, the fire for freedom and nationhood also burned among a faction of the citizenry. History has well recorded them, such as Hamilton and Livingston, and there is no need here to reference them further. But I will mention one, not so well known, but whose breast burned with the same fervor as the others, often referred to as the "Patriot Rabbi." He is Rev. Gershom Mendes Seixas (Say'-shus) Hassan at the Portuguese and Spanish Synagogue on Mill Street, Manhattan. Although not the first synagogue, it was in fact the first building to have been built as a synagogue in North America. His father Isaac had arrived in New York from his native Lisbon three decades earlier, and Gershon was one of his six children. In 1770 Isaac was among the signers of the "Non-Importation Agreement," which was one of the first acts of resistance by the merchants of the Colonies against the oppression of Great Britain.

Gershom took the cloth at an early age. Although never an Ordained Rabbi, he became the beloved

Hassan of his Synagogue where he presided over the services each week. A partisan of the revolutionaries, he fled the city when the British occupied it, and took with him the holy scrolls of the congregation, first to Stanford, Connecticut, and latter to Philadelphia. His brothers were also ardent patriots and served as officers in the Continental Army and state militias.

Returning to New York at the end of the war, he became the leading representative of the Jewish community in the new nation, and was among the religious leaders who were invited to attend the inauguration of President Washington.

painting by John Trumball>

Signing of the Declaration of Independence.

His faith in the new republic can be seen in a reply to a question by Hannah Adams, who had been preparing her two-volume work, *The History of the Jews, From the Destruction of the Temple to the Beginning of the Nineteenth Century*; she asked him to comment on any sufferings from discrimination and civil disabilities toward Jews in America. Expressing indignation at what he saw as an unfair attack on the Republic, Seixas replied that the question, "surprises me very much... as the Constitution of the United States as well as the Constitution of New York does not disqualify any person from holding an office either of honor or trust on account of his religious principles or tenets.... All are entitled to equal rights and privileges.... My dear Madam, there is one thing which I would wish you to notice... that the Justice and righteousness of Providence is manifested in the dispersion of his People... for they have never been driven from any one country without finding an Asylum in another... and this Country... the United States of America, is perhaps the only place where Jews have not suffered persecution but rather the reverse—for through the mercies of a Benign Judge, we are encouraged and indulged with every right of citizenship." (Berman, Howard A, "The First American Jew: A Tribute to Gershom Mendes Seixas 'Patriot Rabbi of the Revolution,'" *Issues,* Spring 2007.

The Battle Begins

Shortly after the arrival of Washington in New York, the Declaration of Independence was signed. It was celebrated in New York by a group of patriots who took the opportunity to bring down the equestrian statue of King George. Being made of gilded lead, it would be given back to the British in the form of musket shot.

While much of the city's population, merchants and aristocrats with strong ties to England, were loyalists—the decision not to hold the city, was for purely topographical reasons. The reality was that it was surrounded by water, and therefore accessible on all sides by the unchallengeable British fleet. New York would not be held, but it was not to be given as a gift to the British, A battle would be fought.

Washington arrived in New York on April 13, 1776, and began gathering what would become an army of nearly 20,000 men, who were neither well-trained nor well-supplied. He set about building his defenses, which rested on three principal locations: the city itself at lower Manhattan, which was fortified; on Long Island, which is now Brooklyn, where a system of defenses were established that centered on the fortification of Brooklyn Heights and what are now the nearby Red Hook and Fort Greene sections of Brooklyn south of Brooklyn Heights, where a fort of that name was erected; and in upper Manhattan in what is now Washington and Harlem Heights. Fort Washington was established at what is now the location of the Manhattan side of the George Washington Bridge, and another fort, Fort Lee, on the New Jersey side. It was hoped that these could prevent the British navy from entering the upper reaches of the Hudson River.

Thus there were three lines of defense: the fortified positions in Brooklyn, the fortified positions in New York City on Lower Manhattan, and the "highlands" of Manhattan beginning at 125 Street, through Harlem Heights, and Washington Heights.

General Howe arrived on June 29 with an initial fleet of 45 warships, which soon increased to 130 including transports and supply ships. He landed on Staten Island with a well-trained army of no less than 32,000 men, including 8,000 Hessian mercenaries, and a fleet grown to 400 warships and transports. They quickly occupied Staten Island.

Five days later they were welcomed with the announcement of the signing of the Declaration of Independence on July 4th, which was duly celebrated under the guns of the British Fleet.

Hoping for a negotiated surrender, Howe sent a letter offering negotiations addressed to "George Washington Esquire" and not "General George Washington"—a display of contempt for our declaration of nationhood. The letter was rejected with the comment that no such man, "George Washington Esquire," was known. This bid for a negotiated surrender failed.

Washington was prepared for battle. He had divided his forces, half behind the Manhattan fortifications and the other half behind those in Brooklyn. To Washington's consternation—for he had been expecting Howe to make his main attack on Manhattan—the British chose to attack Brooklyn first. It should be noted that this British flanking operation was not so much a demonstration of military brilliance by Howe, as in fact the outcome of his fundamental weakness—that being his truly limited resources. Although his army was far superior to that of Washington, and could easily have sustained a vigorous direct assault on Manhattan, he dared not do so. He knew his losses could not easily be replaced. Hessian mercenaries were hugely expensive, and it was not at all clear when he could expect reinforcements.

As luck would have it for Howe, Loyalists in Brooklyn revealed a weak point that lay at the very center of the American line. Making his main attack at that very point, Howe forced the Americans to withdraw behind the fortifications on Brooklyn Heights.

Fearing once again lest he suffer irreplaceable losses, Howe chose to lay siege rather than launch a direct assault. Seeing the opportunity, Washington launched one of those brilliant maneuvers he would become famous for. That very first night, Washington mobilized every available boat and skiff and withdrew all 9,000 men, bringing them across the East River to Manhattan, literally under the guns of the British fleet. With the first light of dawn, the British found to their consternation that the Americans had escaped.

Lamenting the scene of retreat, Howe's deputy Adjutant General, Stephan Kemble, wrote in his diary, "Friday, August 30th. In the morning, to our great astonishment, found [the rebels] had evacuated all their works on Brookland and Red Hook, without a shot being fired at them."

Looking across a sea of concrete, brick and asphalt more than two centuries later, it is hard to imagined the battle of Long Island. Yet small patches of the battlefield can now be tread upon in Greenwood Cemetery, Prospect Park and Fort Greene Park. The resting place of the remains of 11,000 Continental prisoners of war who died in brutal captivity, Fort Greene Park has been truly sanctified as "sacred blood-soaked land."

While Washington had no intention of holding the city, he would not beat too hasty a retreat, for he now realized that Howe was playing an over-cautious game which Washington could use to his advantage in his intention to drag out the battle longer and longer. So Washington would play as if he intended to hold the city while preparing yet another escape.

While a more ambitious general would immediately have prepared for landings on Manhattan, Howe continued his policy of caution. He did not want to destroy the city, because he wanted it as his winter headquarters—so he hoped to maneuver Washington out of New York. Rather than cross over to Manhattan from Brooklyn, Howe moved his forces from Brooklyn to the northwest tip of Long Island in what is now the Greek neighborhood of Astoria in Queens, a move aimed at demonstrating a threat to encircle Washington's forces, and thus forcing the latter to withdraw from the city. In reality, Washington was systematically transferring supplies and men to his next line of defense, Washington Heights, as well as further north to White Plains, in Westchester. Yet to Howe, Washington appeared to be holding fast behind his fortifications on lower Manhattan.

After waiting more than two weeks after his victory

in Brooklyn, and with the approach of winter in mind, Howe finally acted, and following bombardment from his fleet, forced a landing of 9,000 troops at Kips Bay in Manhattan, at what is now the east end of 34th Street, on September 15th. While the American troops at that location made a very feeble, if not disgraceful attempt at defending the beaches, Washington was in fact in the last phase of transferring his army to his northern defenses. Howe found a city empty of all Continental forces. Washington had escaped a certain trap a second time.

While Washington and his commanders discussed whether to burn down the city after with-

drawn by A.R. Waud

The Battle of Harlem Heights, September 16, 1776.

drawing, the Continental Congress advised against it for fear that the British would follow the same practice. Although parts of the city were set afire in what is believed to have been a totally unauthorized move by over-zealous patriots, no city was burned during the revolution.

Setting up his headquarters at the Roger Morris House, a mansion on the landed estate of Colonel Roger Morris, a loyalist who had fled to England, Washington prepared for what would become the Battle of Washington Heights. The Roger Morris House still stands, and thanks to the Daughters of the American Revolution and the city of New York, is preserved as a museum of Washington's headquarters. Built in 1765, the beautiful Georgian-style mansion is the oldest existing house on all of Manhattan.

The house stands at the highest point on Manhattan. In the sense of a topographical feature, Washington Heights is the acropolis of Manhattan. Try to create the scene in your mind's eye, and you will see a spectacular view surrounded by rolling fields and forest and blue water. To the west is the Hudson River and the high Palisades on the New Jersey side; to the north the confluence of the Hudson and Harlem rivers, to the East the expanding Long Island Sound, and to the south New York Harbor. Paying a military compliment to the scene, an unknown British army officer said, "This is a damned strong piece of ground—ten

thousand of our men would defend it against the world."

Following the landing, Howe moved more quickly and began the pursuit of Washington's forces. So arrogant were the British they had their light-infantry buglers sound "Gone Away," a popular fox-hunting call signaling that the fox was in full flight. This proved yet another tactical mistake. It was not only the rage it created among the Continentals, but it betrayed an arrogance that once again Washington would use to steal a small but significant victory in what is known as the Battle of Harlem Heights. That venture, Washington wrote to Patrick Henry at the time, had as its purpose "to recover that military ardour, which is of utmost moment to an army."

The new battle line was 110th Street and 125th Street. To the extreme west of this line on 125th Street is what is known as Manhattan Valley. On the south of the valley is Morningside Heights, and to its north the ground rises to highlands formed by Harlem Heights and Washington Heights, further north. The base of this valley formed what was known as the "Hollow Way."

On September 16, Washington learned that the British were advancing north, including Morningside Heights. Locating himself at the advanced outpost of the American line of defense on the north side of Manhattan Valley, that same day, he ordered a contingent of 150 men under the command of Lt. Col. Thomas Know-

Washington's Retreat on Long Island.

engraved by J.C. Armytage

land to make a probe against the enemy to the north of the valley. As was expected, the force soon encountered a superior force of British light infantry, and a lively skirmish ensued. Seeing an attempt to outflank his greatly inferior forces, Knowland ordered a retreat that was carried out swiftly and in orderly fashion without loss. In their arrogance, the British Buglers again sounded "Gone Away." The British position was then quickly reinforced.

Making a quick estimate of the situation, Washington saw his chance to bloody the nose of the British troops in the very face of their arrogance, in a maneuver Patton once described as "grabbing the enemy by the nose and kicking him in the pants." Regrouping his forces, he deployed 150 men to sally forth in a frontal attack towards the British line. But this was only a feint, to draw out the British forces, who Washington rightly estimated would counter-attack in a flight forward that would ignore the security of their flanks. With the enemy drawn into the Hollow Way, another force was to deploy to strike the advancing force in their rear, in a move Washington hoped would lead to the capture of a large number of British troops.

Although the encircling force struck too soon, hitting the enemy on its flank and not its rear, the operations succeed in forcing the British force into an unorganized and bloody retreat. Seeing the coattails of the fleeing British sent an electrifying remoralization throughout Washington's army.

Despite this victory, Washington had no illusions concerning the weakness of his forces, and his strategy was not to give Howe a decisive defeat—for he knew that was impossible—but to draw out the battle which the British had hoped to win within a number a weeks to end the "rebellion" once and for all. Instead, it would last for months, creating a situation which would be seen across the Atlantic as stiff resistance to King George's best troops by the rebels fighting for a republic.

After the battle of Harlem Heights, while stiffening his defense line on the heights, Washington was also withdrawing forces to White Plains, where Howe had deployed a powerful force in a bid to encircle Washington's position on Manhattan. Nonetheless the affair dragged on for another month of little activity by the British, who did not become active again until Washington had redeployed much of his army out of Manhattan.

But here he learned a bitter lesson. While it was his judgment that Manhattan should be totally evacuated, much like Brooklyn Heights had been, he was prevailed upon by his officers to allow for a protracted stand against the British at Fort Washington. This ended in disaster. The British were able to quickly surround the fort, and its commander, Colonel Robert Magaw, soon surrendered his command of over two thousand men, many of whom would not survive their captivity.

Nonetheless Washington gave battle to Howe in White Plains, retreated in good order, crossed the Hudson into New Jersey, and headed in the direction of Pennsylvania along a line of withdrawal prepared beforehand. It was now November. A battle that should have ended in a matter of days, was instead drawn out into a campaign of four months. For the British, the first year of the revolution was not a happy one. Their evacuation of Boston in the spring of 1776 in the face of the siege mounted by Washington, was followed by a four-month campaign to capture New York, a city that Washington had no intention of keeping—only to see Washington and his Continental Army escape to fight another day.

Part II will appear in next week's issue.

Tribute to Sylvia Olden Lee, Master Musician and Teacher

June 27—Executive Intelligence Review *received the following press announcement, regarding the remembrance of Sylvia Lee (1917-2004), the great voice coach and accompanist, and member of the cultural advisory board of the Schiller Institute, whose 100th Birthday would have been this June 29.*

"The Foundation for the Revival of Classical Culture is pleased to announce that the Mayor's Office of the City of New York will issue a proclamation that will declare June 29th to be 'Sylvia Olden Lee Day.' Sylvia Olden Lee was a great artist and a pioneer of the Metropolitan Opera. A self-proclaimed 'granddaughter of a slave,' Sylvia was instrumental in giving African-Americans access to the Metropolitan stage for the first time. She lived in New York City for many years. Her achievements live on in the work of the Harlem Opera Theatre and many musical institutions and persons. She is a truly great 'hidden figure' who deserves this recognition."

EIR notes that the proclamation is to be presented at the Foundation's commemorative program at Carnegie Hall on June 29. Tribute statements were received from many, including artists Jessye Norman, George Shirley, Bobby McFerrin, and many others. Sylvia Lee spent many hours, together with her friend, the great bass-baritone Bill Warfield, working with members of Schiller Institute choruses in the 1990s, touring Europe and the United States on behalf of her Project SYLVIA (Saving Young Lyric Voices In Advance), and in the creation of a new audience for Classical music.

Two of those tribute statements appear below, including that issued by Helga Zepp-LaRouche, President and Founder of the German Schiller Institute. Sylvia Lee spent many hours in the company of Helga and Lyndon LaRouche, including at their home. She was particularly intrigued by the LaRouches' project to return Classical musical performance, especially vocal

Sylvia Olden Lee
1917-2004

performance, to the "Verdi tuning" of C=256 Hz, requiring an "A" with a range between 427-432 Hz, far lower than the modern "A" which ranges from 440 to 450 Hz on the modern opera stage.

Greeting from Schiller Institute Founder and President Helga Zepp-LaRouche

Sylvia Olden Lee was one of those absolutely outstanding artists who are capable of crystalizing the essence of a piece of music, the true idea, only accessible to those individuals who can read the intention of the poet and the composer. She implanted throughout her life, in the many pupils and people she inspired, the knowledge of how the artist, the singer, or the instrumentalist steps modestly behind the composition, but at the same time adds his or her ennobled individuality to the performance, to make it both unique and absolutely truthful.

In doing that, she was always playful, polemical, full of humor, profound, loving, and with a disarming openness, and by representing all of these characteristics, she would liberate her students, as well as the audience, out of their normal unelevated condition to the higher plane of true art. She was able, like only a few, to let those around her participate directly in the creative process, in the diligent work of the kind of perfection it takes to actually produce art, as opposed to only making nice sounds.

The afternoons and evenings when she would participate in a *Musikabende* or coaching sessions in our place in Virginia, together with William Warfield, Robert McFerrin, and numerous other classical artists, belong to the fondest memories for my husband, Lyndon LaRouche, and myself. Sylvia and Bill were for many years on the board of the Schiller Institute and added an invaluable treasure to its work.

In thinking about Sylvia, one suddenly wishes she

were still here, since what she taught is so very needed for humanity.

A Centennial Celebration of the Life of Sylvia Olden Lee
Eugene Thamon Simpson, Ed.D.

Any centennial celebration of the life of Sylvia Olden Lee must be a retrospective of her origin, her education, her work, her influence, and the lives she touched. Although she loved the phrase, "born as the granddaughter of slaves," Sylvia Olden was born into a privileged family in Meridian, Mississippi on June 29, 1917. Her father, James Olden, a Minister, and her mother, Sylvia Ward, were both graduates of Fisk University where her father had been a tenor in the Fisk Quartet with Roland Hayes, and her mother, a singer of such excellence that she was offered a contract at the Metropolitan Opera in 1913 if she would pass as white. Little Sylvia proved to be a prodigy, accompanying her parents by the age of eight, and playing in concerts from the age of ten. Her precocity attracted the attention of many in high places, and she was invited to play at the White House for President Roosevelt's first Inauguration, and later by Mrs. Roosevelt in 1942. After two years at Howard University, Ms. Olden was offered, and accepted, a full scholarship to Oberlin Conservatory from which she graduated with honors in 1938, with a major in piano performance. Her musical and linguistic abilities were further developed by a Fulbright Scholarship for study at the Accademia Nazionale di Santa Cecilia in Rome, seven years in Germany during which she studied German *Lieder* and opera, and seven years in Sweden, where she coached and performed with her husband, violinist and conductor, Everett Lee.

Before moving to Europe in 1956, Sylvia taught at Talladega College, Dillard University, and Howard University; she toured the southern states with singer Paul Robeson; and she accompanied singers in the voice studios of Elizabeth Schumann, Eva Gautier, Konrad Bos, Rosalie Miller, Fritz Lehmann, and many others. She coached singers for New York City Opera, the Tanglewood Festival, and in 1954, became the first African American on the coaching staff of the Metropolitan Opera as a Kathryn Tourney Long Scholar. It is to her activist intervention with Max Rudolph and Rudolph Bing that we attribute the debut of Marian Anderson as the first of her race to sing from the Metropolitan Opera stage. This opened the door for Robert McFerrin, Leon-

tyne Price, and all who followed. In 1970, Mrs. Lee returned to Philadelphia to join the faculty of the Curtis Institute as a Vocal Coach, a position she would hold until 1990. She coached the singers for the Metropolitan Opera premiere of *Porgy and Bess*, for the Russian production of the same opera, and for the Carnegie Hall "Spirituals in Concert" with James Levine.

Sylvia Lee's influence can best be measured by the principal singers she has worked with. A greatly abbreviated list would include scores of emerging artists at the institutions of higher education, at the Metropolitan Opera, New York City Opera, and at Curtis, as well as a bevy of stars including Kathleen Battle, Jessye Norman, Marian Anderson, Robert McFerrin, Grace Bumbry, and Simon Estes. While much of her work involved coaching and playing the standard classical operatic and art song repertoire, her long association with the Schiller Institute took her to many colleges and universities to conduct master classes on the African American Spiritual, alone, and with William Warfield. One year before her death on April 10, 2004, Oberlin Conservatory conferred upon her an Honorary Doctor of Music Degree.

I shall never forget her fearlessness and musical competence which she demonstrated at the Hall Johnson Centennial Festival, which I produced at Rowan University (then Glassboro State College) in 1988. It was a three-day retrospective of the life and works of Hall Johnson that featured headliners Jester Hairston, William Warfield, Leonard De Paur, D. Antoinette Handy, three choral concerts, and five solo recitals of Hall Johnson's music. One day before the festival was to begin, John Motley, former accompanist for Marian Anderson, who was scheduled to play for John Morrison (then tenor soloist at Riverside Church), and Dr. Blanche Foreman (a former pupil of mine who was then on the faculty at Vassar), cancelled for personal reasons. Morrison's recital was of Hall Johnson's original art songs, and Foreman's of familiar Spirituals. Without batting an eye, Sylvia, who had been hired to play recitals for Gregory Hopkins and Barbara Dever, stepped in, and with only a single rehearsal, played John Morrison's recital admirably and to the enthusiastic acclaim of the audience. I played Dr. Foreman's recital which also delighted the audience. Both performances are preserved on the 4-CD album, *The Best of the Hall Johnson Centennial Festival*. I shall forever be grateful to her for her help in rescuing the festival and for her contribution to the performances of those rarely heard, and not previously recorded, works. "Thank you, Sylvia." You live on in our memory and in these performances.

U.S. Will Cooperate with China on Belt and Road Initiative, Trump Says

by William Jones

June 23—U.S. President Donald Trump met with Chinese State Councillor Yang Jiechi on June 22. State Councillor Yang, who had served for many years as China's Ambassador to the United States, was in Washington, together with General Fang Fenghui, the chief of staff of the People's Liberation Army, for the first meeting of the Diplomatic and Security Dialogue. President Trump told Yang, "The United States is willing to cooperate with China on relevant projects under the Belt and Road Initiative"—the clearest statement he has yet made on the United States joining the Belt and Road.

Xinhua

Chinese State Councilor Yang Jiechi met President Donald Trump in Washington, D.C. June 22, 2017. Yang Jiechi attended the first session of the China-U.S. Diplomatic and Security Dialogue, a new, high-level framework for negotiations that was launched by President Trump and China President Xi Jinping.

Yang visited the White House the day after the first session of the Diplomatic and Security Dialogue, one of four dialogues set up by President Trump during his meeting with President Xi in April. The dialogues are intended to become high-level forums between China and the United States to create concrete outcomes for the relationship, as it moves forward. The other dialogues cover Economics, Law Enforcement and Cyber-Security, and Social and Cultural Exchanges.

Yang went to the White House for meetings with National Security Adviser H.R. McMasters and Presidential Adviser and Trump son-in-law, Jared Kushner. But there he also met with President Trump himself. General Fang Fenghui was also present at that meeting. Trump told Yang that he and President Xi Jinping had had a successful meeting in Mar-a-Lago and reached important consensus. He said that it was gratifying to see that the cooperation between the United States and China has made positive progress since their meeting.

Yang told Trump that China greatly appreciated the U.S. attendance at the May 14-15 Belt and Road Forum, and would be willing to work with the United States on the initiative. Yang also said that President Xi was looking forward to meeting with the U.S. President next month at the G24 Meeting in Germany, and then, later in the year, on a state visit to China. Yang also extended an invitation to Ivanka Trump, the President's daughter, and to Kushner, to visit China before the state visit, to which the President agreed.

Trump's statement is the most explicit that the President has made regarding this project, although very much consistent with everything else he has done since the meeting with Xi in Florida April 6-7. At that meeting, President Trump had agreed to send a U.S. delegation to the Belt and Road Forum in Beijing, which President Xi had taken the initiative to organize, in order to consolidate international support for this major infrastructure project.

China was invited to attend the June 18-20 SelectUSA Summit in Washington, a U.S. government investment promotion program which brings together people in government and industry in an attempt to spur economic growth. This year's event, attended by a record 1,200 foreign guests, also included an unprecedented 155-person delegation from China. State Councillor Yang, fully aware of the way Washington works, also spent time on Capitol Hill, meeting with House

Speaker Paul Ryan, among others. Yang proposed that there be more exchanges between the two legislatures to promote greater understanding. Yang also met with Senator Bob Corker, the chairman of the Senate Foreign Relations Committee.

Relations over the Next 40 Years

The growing ties between the two countries were also in evidence at the meeting of the Diplomatic and Security Dialogue. At its conclusion, Secretary of State Rex Tillerson and Defense Secretary James Mattis met the press. "U.S. and China relations have undergone a profound transformation over the past 40 years," Tillerson said, adding,

> These dialogues provide an opportunity to consider how we're going to engage and how we're going to live with one another over the next 40 years. In furthering this relationship, we need to work to expand areas of cooperation, as we did today, on issues where we have shared security interest.

While the two had discussed issues on which there is a good deal of agreement, such as achieving a nuclear-free Korean Peninsula, as well as issues on which they have significant differences, as on the South China Sea, the emphasis was on charting the way forward over the next 40 years. "An important part of our discussion about the next 40 years was increasing mutual trust and working toward a long-term risk reduction effort between our two militaries and our governments," Tillerson said. He continued,

Xinhua/Chen Jianli

Matthew Pottinger, U.S. Special Assistant to the President and National Security Council Senior Director for Asian Affairs, speaks at Thematic Session on Infrastructure Connectivity of the Belt and Road Forum (BRF) for International Cooperation in Beijing, China, May 14, 2017.

> Building on what we've done in the air and maritime spaces, U.S. and Chinese civilian and military teams will start discussions in new areas of strategic concern like space, cyberspace, nuclear forces, and nonproliferation issues. We need to enhance stability and develop strong international standards in these areas, and we need China to play a major role.

In line with that, Secretary Mattis announced that the United States and China would—

> explore new areas of military-to-military cooperation, including exchange of officers to improve transparency and mutual understanding.

> The two sides agreed to arrange mutual visits by defense ministers at an early date, as well as a visit to China by the U.S. Chairman of the Joint Chiefs of Staff.

> During the meeting, the U.S. side said that it understands that China is undergoing rapid development, and the U.S. does not have any intention to rein in or weaken China. Instead, it stands ready to develop a long-term and constructive relationship with China.

U.S. Dept of State/youtube

After the Diplomatic and Security Dialog with China, Defense Secretary James Mattis (Left) and Secretary of State Rex Tillerson addressed the press.

Trump's 100-Day Plan Is On Schedule

Meanwhile, what is happening at the highest levels of government has been followed up by a steady stream of delegations coming to the United States to build further on the new relationship between the two leaders. A recent delegation, headed by Zhao Qizheng, the former head of the Information Office of the State Council, visited Iowa, where the home in which President Xi stayed as a young official studying agriculture, is now a museum. President Xi had come to an agreement with President Trump at Mar-a-Lago that China would again begin to purchase U.S. beef, while the U.S. would import chickens from China. Many Chinese companies are now interested in creating a mechanism for such purposes.

Another delegation, including Zhao Qizheng and former Hong Kong Administrator Tung Chee-hwa, traveled to New York June 14 to discuss with business leaders, at a forum sponsored by the Asia Society, the possibility of increasing investment in each other's country. These were meetings in which Schiller Institute representatives also took an active part. Meetings between Chinese and U.S. scholars were also held the same week by the National Committee on U.S.-China Relations, at which Chinese representatives also underlined the importance of the Belt and Road for such an important financial center like New York.

At the same time, members of the U.S. Chamber of Commerce were in Beijing for discussions with their Chinese counterparts. The U.S. Chamber of Commerce and the China Center for International Economic Exchanges, a Beijing-based think tank staffed by a number of retired senior government officials, said in a joint statement June 21 that the two nations can engage in full cooperation under the Belt and Road Initiative and through a number of other means, including the Asian Infrastructure Investment Bank, World Bank, and other multilateral investment and financing institutions. The conference consisted of CEOs from many American companies interested in investing in China.

This increased level of activity is also occurring with an eye toward the completion of the 100-day economic cooperation plan, initiated by the Trump Administration to significantly upgrade U.S.-China economic relations within that period. On July 16, all of the new agreements on trade and investment are scheduled to be in place for bringing the trade and investment relationship to a new level.

'The U.S.A. and Russia in the Arctic'

by Michael Billington

June 22—As the dying breed of neoconservatives—both the Republican leadership and the Obama/Hillary wing of the Democrats—is acting more and more hysterically and dangerously every day to stop President Donald Trump from realizing his stated intention of forming a friendly and cooperative agreement with Russia and President Putin, a two-day forum held in Washington's Wilson Center on June 21 and 22 was a breath of fresh air, and an important strategic intervention into the hostile environment in the nation's capital.

The Wilson Center, together with the Arctic Circle, an NGO of scientific, political, and business people involved in the development of the Arctic, sponsored the two-day forum, titled *The U.S. and Russia in the Arctic,* offering powerful insights from multiple perspectives on the urgency of maintaining the existing close cooperation between the United States and Russia in the Arctic.

More important, most of the speakers—from both Arctic nations and others who recognize the growing importance of the Arctic for world development—called for the existing close and critical cooperation of the U.S.A. and Russia in the Arctic, to serve more broadly as a model and an impetus for the restoration of ties between the two great nations.

The Arctic Circle's initiator Olafur Grimsson, the former President of Iceland (who stood up to the Anglo-Dutch banks in 2012, and won), Wilson President Jane Harman, and Alaska Senator Lisa Murkowski gave opening presentations, making

clear that the intent of the event was not only to advance cooperation in the Arctic, but to bring the United States and Russia together for international peace and development. While there were objections to this from a few speakers, most added their own support for this broader, urgent necessity.

Grimsson praised the U.S. chairmanship of the Arctic Council over the past two years (the Arctic Council is composed of government representatives from the eight Arctic countries—Finland is now taking the chair), noting that the United States had "significant help from Russia," demonstrating that the two countries "can have a very constructive and successful relationship."

Jane Harman added that it was important that this conference was being held in Washington, since "most members of Congress know nothing about the Arctic." She said that the close cooperation with Russia in the Arctic "builds a bridge" between the two nations.

Sen. Murkowski, who serves also on the Standing

photo courtesy of Novatek

Liquefied natural gas plant and sea port at Sabetta on Russia's Yamal Peninsula.

Committee of Arctic Parliamentarians, called for "taking this positive relationship here [in the Arctic] to impact broader U.S.-Russia relations." She said that co-operation between Secretary Tillerson and Foreign Minister Lavrov at the Arctic Council meeting in Fairbanks this past May facilitated an agreement on scientific cooperation in the Arctic. She also noted that Russia is far ahead of the United States in building the necessary infrastructure for Arctic development and for facilitating the Northern Passage, which is now far more accessible and important because of the dramatic recession of the Arctic ice cap.

Sen. Murkowski—and many others—noted that the United States once had seven icebreakers, and now has one, with another in dry dock. The South Korean Ambassador for Arctic Affairs, Kim Young-jun, who spoke later, said that his country had recently presented the first of 15 Korean-built LNG tanker/icebreakers to Russia. Others noted that Russia, Finland, and other countries are also producing icebreakers, while none have been funded in the United States—a sign of strategic and economic insanity.

One panel included the former Lt. Gov. of Alaska Mead Treadwell (a close associate of former Gov. Hickel, a pioneer in Arctic development), together with Russian Senator Igor Chernyshenko, who represents the Murmansk Oblast on the Arctic. Chernyshenko praised the work of the Arctic Council under U.S. chairmanship over the past two years, pointing out that there is no potential for conflict, now, in the Arctic. He said, bad relations between the United States and Russia at this time were "due to the moods in the Congress." He described some of the 140 projects underway in the Arctic, including the huge Yamal gas and oil port, rail development, and other projects, noting the significant Chinese involvement (there were no Chinese participants in the event). He encouraged the United States and others to engage in the Russian projects, noting that the opening of the Northeast passage facilitates participation of all nations, not just the Arctic nations, adding that current tensions are forcing U.S. companies to lose out on great potentials.

Lt. Gov. Treadwell also called for U.S. cooperation with Russia, proposing a "League of Arctic Ports," to, among other things, facilitate expanded container traffic through the passage. He noted China's New Silk Road projects and their huge investments, calling on the U.S. government to engage in funding and infrastructure development in the region.

LaRouche and Putin—2007

In the Q&A session, *EIR* referenced the 2007 Moscow forum on building a tunnel under the Bering Strait, noting that President Putin described the project as a "war avoidance" policy, building a physical connection between the United States and Russia based on the mutual intersts of each. *EIR* noted that a paper by Lyndon LaRouche was presented at that conference, but that except for Alaskan Gov. Hickel, there has been no significant U.S. response to Putin's offer. *EIR* asked if it were not even more urgent now to proceed with this beneficial project.

Treadwell answered that his friend Gov. Hickel had often said that the Bering Strait Tunnel "will not happen in my lifetime, but we must keep talking about it every day." He said that every project, big or small, to drive cooperation with Russia, was extremely important, and described a joint ship-monitoring system now being developed for the Bering Sea. Treadwell also pointed to the recent agreement to pursue building a rail connection from the lower 48 states through Canada to Alaska, and noted that such a rail line could eventually reach the Bering Strait and proceed on to Russia via a tunnel.

Treadwell and others noted that China has now declared the city of Dalian to be its "Arctic port," and that the United States needs to quickly develop a deep water Arctic port on the north shore of Alaska.

Congressman Don Young (R-Alaska) decried the fact that "our media peddles the idea that Russia is our enemy—there is no reason." He said that the Arctic is our future.

Develop the Arctic—Develop Outer Space

Georgy Karlov, the Deputy Chairman of the Duma representing Sakhalin, said that developing the Arctic is like developing space, both because the technological challenges are similar in many respects, but also because the harsh conditions mean that no country can do it alone, that all nations need to cooperate. "The United States and the Russians went to space separately, but now they have learned that they must work closely together."

Kathleen Crane, the coordinator of the Russian-American Long-term Census of the Arctic (RUSALCA) —Rusalca means mermaid in Russian—spoke on the close cooperation of Russian and American scientists in mapping the Arctic since the founding of RUSALCA in 2003, but at the same time expressed her sorrow that the sanctions have to a large extent, now, undermined their mission.

It's Time to Leave the Valley of the Clueless: Watch 'The Putin Interviews'

by Rachel Brown

June 26—U.S. statesman Lyndon LaRouche has often cited the role of the leadership of Russian President Vladimir Putin as providing a crucial strategic factor in current world affairs. "The Putin Interviews," Oliver Stone's recent 20 hours of discussion with the Russian leader available on "Showtime," gives many valuable examples of just how this is the case, and how it is that creative interventions and long-term thinking are the principles which always guide actually successful action among nations.

Not to be forgotten in Putin's strategic thinking is his close personal connection to the defeat of fascism; during the brutal Nazi siege of Leningrad, his older brother died of starvation and his mother was left for dead, only to be revived by Putin's father. These memories are one of Putin's driving forces as a leader, and are deeply connected with his love for his country and its people.

Now take a mental step to another location: the area in East Germany around Dresden, located in the Elbe Valley, known in post-World-War-II history as "The Valley of the Clueless," because television signals from West Germany were not able to enter the area, and residents were virtually clueless as to the goings-on in the outside world, other than what was provided by East German media propaganda. Today, 320 million Americans are living in our own "Valley of the Clueless," as the reality of the world outside has been left "at the door" so to speak, ignored by all significant media outlets.

Putin's interviews provide

OLIVER STONE'S THE PUTIN INTERVIEWS

wikipedia

today's American a vantage point by which to attain a more truthful experience of the world. Many issues are addressed in a manner outside the current "narrative," with a plethora of insightful glimpses into the quality of creative thinking which LaRouche has frequently cited in Putin's personality.

On Creativity, *Per Se*

A few segments shed light on Putin's personal sense of the need for creativity in statecraft. In the first interview, Stone asks Putin, "Your theory of life, they say, is summed up in the philosophy of Judo?" Putin answers, "Yes, more or less. The main idea—the flexible way, as it were—that is the main idea in Judo. You must be flexible. Sometimes you can give way to others. If that is the way leading to victory." The patience exemplified by Putin in resisting hasty responses to numerous provocations, such as the Turkish shooting down of a Russian plane over Syria, or continual personal attacks, are examples of pursuing a path above emotional reaction or immediate gratification, toward greater future victory.

In a later interview, Stone asks Putin a personal question:

Stone: I was speaking to my producer who's here, Fernando—we were talking about you earlier, and he said you are an excellent CEO, Chief Executive Officer of a company—Russia is your company. You kick the tires, you deal with these problems and you try to solve them on the spot. Let's say the problem is this, and you go into the detail here, and the detail gets smaller, and you do a micro detail, and the micro detail has another micro detail, and before you know it you've lost the forest for the trees as they say. That could be very irritating—you could probably go to bed at night not having solved some of these things and it really drives you nuts.

Vladimir Putin: It's not about unresolved issues; it's about the very process of resolving those issues. I try to make it more creative. Just imagine a painter is working and it's dinnertime, and he just quits his picture and goes to dinner. [Pauses.] But that's not how it happens. The painter tries to complete something, and only after that, is he ready to have some rest.

Stone: [To translator] He says he needs to complete something?

Putin: Yes, I have to have this sense of completion. I am not trying to compare myself to a creative professional, but the search for answers is similar in process to what creative professionals do.

Compare this to the method of a Bush, Obama, or Hillary Clinton, who were fully committed to carrying out policies of regime change and perpetual war on behalf of the British empire, and you see why Putin is under attack today. A great leader must think like an artist, or a great general in war, who can act on the basis of a future effect by implementing a creative hypothesis that changes the field of activity.

The Threat of Nuclear War

The defining characteristic of the U.S.-Russian relationship since 1945 has been the threat of global nuclear war. As opposed to the attitude of some British-run U.S. strategists who choose to remain ignorant of the implications of their "playing with fire," or even some who think a nuclear war against Russia would be winnable, Putin demonstrates a sober understanding of the reality presented by a world with nuclear weapons. He repeatedly called for the joint development of missile defense systems, as Lyndon LaRouche had also proposed with his Strategic Defense Initiative, which President Reagan adopted in 1983.

In this interview, on July 4th, they are taking a walk in a wooded, sunny area.

Stone: In a hot war, is the U.S. dominant, yes or no?
Putin: No.

Stone: No. It would be a case of Russia surviving it?
Putin: [Gravely.] I don't think anyone would survive such a conflict.

Stone: [Considers the weight of this statement.] Even with the missile shield...?
Putin: As of now, a missile shield would not protect the entire territory of the United States. There is a threat deriving from the illusion of being protected, and this might lead to more aggressive behavior. That is why it is so important to prevent unilateral actions. That is why we propose to work jointly on the anti-ballistic missile system.

Putin later provides an unexpected, and probably to most observers, shocking description of U.S.-Russian relations after the death of FDR.

Putin says to Stone: Who gave the intelligence regarding nuclear weapon research in the United States to the Soviets after World War II?

Putin continued: "The scientists themselves—those who developed the atomic bomb. Why did they do that? Because they understood the dangers. They let the genie out of the bottle [with emphasis] and now the genie cannot be put back. And this international team of scientists—I think they were more intelligent than the politicians. They provided this information to the Soviet Union of their own volition to restore the nuclear balance in the world. And what are we doing right now? We're trying to destroy this balance. And that's a great mistake."

There have been several overt violations by the United States, under British command, of the global strategic balance. One was the decision by the United States to withdraw from the Anti-Ballistic Missile Treaty, which Putin states was "the cornerstone of the system of national security as a whole. It was the foundation of international security." He described the violation of the promise not to expand NATO after the dissolution of the Soviet Union:

Stone: I mean from what I've heard from Mr. Gorbachov, as well as read from American officials including James Baker, there was a deal with the Soviet Union not to expand NATO eastward.
Putin: Yes, I talked about that publicly—including in Munich [in 2007]. And when the decision was made on the reunification of Germany, back then, the dignitaries both in the United States and the United Nations

Secretary General, and the representative of the Federal Republic of Germany—they were all saying there was one thing that the Soviet Union could be sure of—that the eastern border of NATO would not be extended any further than the eastern border of the German Democratic Republic.

Putin's remarks at that Munich Security Conference have frequently been interpreted as anti-American, which is not true, as he made clear.

'Democracy Can Not Be Imported'

The Putin-Stone interchange is an important complement to the current U.S. shift away from the 16 years of Bush-Obama policy of perpetual war.

Putin elaborates further his thinking in 2007 in Munich, and now.

"I thought it was unacceptable what the United States was doing. And I said we saw what was happening and that we had to take measures. I was saying that we would not let ourselves be dragged to the slaughterhouse and applaud that at the same time. ...

"I just want to emphasize that that approach is dangerous. ... I told you that democracy could not be exported. It cannot be imported from outside. It has to emerge from within society. And this work is more promising even though it is more difficult; it requires patience, it requires much time, and it requires attention. Certainly it's easier to send bombers. And what then? What comes next? And then a surge of terrorism and the need to take the next step to fight terrorism. Take ISIS. Where do they recruit new members? [Putin is referring to Stone's question about U.S. attacks on Libya, Iraq, and Syria.] There are many countries sending people there."

Stone's interview of Putin should remind us that "regime-change" policies have done nothing to better the nations involved or increase world safety. Terrorism has only increased with the covert support of British policies over the recent two decades. The way to improve the lives of citizens is not through externally enforced "democracy," but by creating stability in the world through economic cooperation and the development of basic infrastructure and culture. China and Russia, in partnership with many other countries through the Belt and Road Initiative (New Silk Road), the BRICS, the Shanghai Cooperation Organization, and other international initiatives, have clearly identified and are acting on this concept.

On the New Silk Road

Oliver Stone raised the subject of the New Silk Road with President Putin. Putin highlighted one of the perhaps unintended consquences of Western sanctions against Russia, its turn toward the East.

Putin told Stone that "the so-called sanctions introduced by the West simply pushed this process forward. ... We also have plans for developing the so-called trans-Siberian Railroad and the trans-Baikal Railroad, and it all corresponds well to the Chinese plans for reviving the Silk Road."

On Looking into the Future

The attitude of the U.S. media towards Russia is increasingly hostile, and many Congressmen have sought to paint themselves as better patriots by denouncing Putin or calling for actions against Russia (which could lead to nuclear war). One example was Sen. McCain's call for a Senate veto against the cancellation of Russian sanctions by President Trump. To this, Putin responded:

"People with such convictions as the Senator you mentioned—they still live in the Old World. And they're reluctant to look into the future; they are unwilling to recognize how fast the world is changing. They do not see the real threat, and they cannot leave behind the past which is always dragging them back.

"We supported the U.S. fight for independence. We were allies during World War I and World War II. Right now there are common threats we are both facing, like international terrorism. We've got to fight poverty across the world, and the environmental deterioration which is the real threat to all humanity. After all, we've piled up so many nuclear weapons that it has become a threat to the whole world as well. And it would be good for us to give it some thought."

These interviews underline the reality that the paradigm must be changed. Overcoming the seemingly insurmountable mode of continual conflict, both within the United States and in its relations to other countries, can be achieved only by looking at the world as a whole, by facing the inevitable threat of nuclear war which will erupt if it is not overcome through mutual development. We must take up the repeated offers of cooperation to the United States by the two most important countries in the world—Russia and China. Putin has demonstrated he is already acting for the future—for the next 25 to 100 years. The United States must act on this intention as well.

New British Ambassador to South Africa Leads Regime Change Effort

by Ramasimong Phillip Tsokolibane, leader of LaRouche South Africa

June 22—As the leader of the LaRouche movement in South Africa and as a patriot, I issue the following warning: Beware Perfidious Albion! The Brits have deployed a specialist in regime change operations as their High Commissioner (ambassador) to South Africa.

I have received an intelligence memo, prepared by a qualified associate of mine, which details the career of Britain's new High Commissioner, Mr. Nigel Casey, who has been at his post here since at least April 18. Mr. Casey is a trusted operative of Her Majesty's government, moving in his career as a diplomat through postings which also appear to include management of the type of covert operations which have been deployed by the Queen Bitch against the "troublesome" government of President Zuma, with its visible support for the anti-imperial policies of peace and development espoused by both President Xi of China and President Putin of Russia.

Most notable is Mr. Casey's role in an attempted regime change in Bosnia and Herzegovina while Ambassador there from August 2011 through January 2014; the fruit of his efforts was seen less than a month after he left, when bloody violence erupted in Tuzla. The Brits would like to engineer a similar result in our nation, plunging it into bloody chaos and making it ungovernable, as a way to stop motion in our country towards the new global order being ushered in by the Chinese and Russians, to replace the decadent and dying British Empire-dominated global monetarist system.

The deployment of Mr. Casey to South Africa is not surprising on a number of counts. For one thing, the Zuma government, whose leader the Brits privately (and occasionally, publicly) ridicule, has so far stymied an elaborate and continuing regime change operation against it. We have witnessed the open support of that regime change operation from the U.S. Administration of British asset Barack Obama. And we have been the target of the Nazi-loving billionaire speculator George Soros through his various front organizations. Now,

UK High Commission, Pretoria

The new British High Commissioner in Pretoria, Nigel Casey.

with Washington moving in a different direction under the new American President Donald Trump, London must take charge of the regime change operation in its own name.

So much the better for patriots of this nation. It makes clear who we are fighting—the British Empire. It should give you further impetus to heed the call that I have been making for some time: that we finally take our feet out of the dirty backwaters of the British Empire, and move fully into the new expansive sea of change that is the BRICS alliance and China's Belt and Road Initiative. Delaying such actions will only give Mr. Casey and his minions more time to work their deadly mischief.

If there should be any surprises that open the door for regime change, lay the blame on Mr. Casey and the Brits. But why wait for that? Far better, shut the whole operation down now! Pull out of the Commonwealth, and cut our ties with Perfidious Albion! You have been warned.

ramasimongt@hotmail.com

III. The Genius Shapes History

Dante Alighieri and the New Paradigm for Human Culture

by Robert Ingraham

If you can't speak of the future of mankind, you ain't serious—you're just babbling.
                                        —Lyndon LaRouche, April 12, 2017

Preface

June 26—The human species is blessed with a universal identity, a universal species-nature. For more than sixty years, Lyndon LaRouche has defended that unique universality of the human identity against all challengers: the singular *agapic* creative nature of the human mind which is universal for every member of the human race, that quality of profound love and profound creativity which defines mankind's mission in the universe.

On May 14-15, 2017 more than one hundred nations took part in the One Belt One Road Forum in Beijing, China. Among the participants were twenty-eight heads of state, including those of China, Russia, Indonesia, Turkey, Greece, and the Philippines. A close examination of those who participated in Beijing and those now engaged in this noble effort to eliminate the dying vestiges of imperial rule, reveals that among the new allies there exists a kaleidoscope of cultures, histories, religions, and races. Every shade and hue of the human race was represented in Beijing. Language groups representing widely divergent ways of articulating human expression were in dialogue. Many of the nations involved have a long history of past rivalries, jealousies, and hostilities, which for some are not merely memories, but exist as areas of mistrust and conflict down to the present day.

The challenge—in the post-imperial era—is to redefine the relations among nations, cultures, and peoples throughout the world. Helga Zepp-LaRouche, the chairwoman of the Schiller Institute, has stated the urgent need for a Dialogue of Civilizations. She has already initiated this effort, stressing the beneficial results which might result from an examination of what has been, historically, the best in these cultures, the high points, the renaissances. It is hoped that from such an effort will flow a deeper appreciation of those principles and those beliefs which are common to all, those universal principles which have advanced human civilization in many different parts of the world over millennia.

It is precisely that desire which motivates this current work on Dante Alighieri. There are those—particularly among the Anglo-American elite—who would shatter and fragment the human identity. Under the

Helga Zepp-LaRouche participated in the Belt and Road Forum for International Cooperation.

guise of modern-day existentialist "cultural relativism," they proclaim that mankind is eternally divided by widely divergent cultures, with different religions, philosophies, and values. In their view, perhaps a syncretism of ethically acceptable "shared values" might allow different nations to "co-exist," but always within a geometry of divided, competing interests. They propose a perpetual Tower of Babel, in which people and nations become pawns to be profiled and manipulated.

We aim for something far better: a world in which the true nature of our species may flourish and the principle of the human identity, as understood by Dante, shall become the guiding light for future generations.

Introduction

Today, and throughout the 20th Century, everything that Dante Alighieri stood for has been under assault. The academic journals are filled with articles dissecting almost every aspect of his life, his beliefs, and his literary work, but the real Dante will not be found there. A moral indifference permeates these writings, and Jonathan Swift's Laputans show more sense than some of these characters. The worst aspect to so-called "Dante Studies" is reflected in the deference given to the likes of Ezra Pound, T.S. Eliot, and other 20th Century existentialists and fascists as to their "authority" on the subject of Dante's poetic method. It is as if Lucifer were appointed to stand judge over the Divine.

The issue at hand is to grasp the reality of the upward, self-directed evolution of humanity, and to ask the question, "How has this been possible?" This is the relevant subject matter in considering Dante. This gets to the heart of Dante's examination of the Human Mind. It is not enough to simply stand in awe of his poetic skills. A courageous approach to Dante, of this type, promises great benefits to the work before us today.

For those who have never invesigated the writings of Dante, I implore you to take the plunge. Dive into the deep end. From his poetry and his writings on language and the vernacular in *La Vita Nuova* (The New Life) and *De Vulgari Eloquentia* (On Eloquence in the Vernacular), to his poetic and philosophical *Convivio* (The Banquet), to his masterpiece on government and society, *De Monarchia* (On Monarchy), and, ultimately, to his "divine" *Commedia*, Dante made possible everything great that subsequently arose in 15th Century Florence, and it is the monumental repercussions of those breakthroughs in human culture which persist down to the present day.

I will not recommend any specific translation. Dante himself warned, "Nothing that is harmonized by the laws of poetry can be changed from its own language to another without destroying all its sweetness and harmony." I have studied numerous translations of Dante into English, from the 19th Century efforts of Cayley, Cary, and Longfellow to the spate of more recent translations (Binyon, Sayer, Ciardi, Mandelbaum, the Hollanders, and others). Some have great strengths; all of them have weaknesses. In truth, translating Dante's Italian poetry and the idea-content of his mind into modern-day English is an impossible task, and the vocation of the translator is most unenviable. Just find one you like and start reading!

One word of warning: Only those who share Dante's life mission to change the conditions of the world, and to create revolutionary, new potentials within human society for future generations, will understand what he writes. Those who sit on the sidelines, watching passively the decay of the society around them, will understand nothing. Such individuals are only fit to be judged by Dante and put in the appropriate circle of the *Inferno*.

I. Historical Specificity

An egregious flaw in much of modern historiography is to take people and events out of their own time. Although Dante's is an immortal mind with a universal message, it is impossible to consider what he did and what he wrote, without understanding the era and the realities with which he was confronted.

Dante lived from 1265 to 1321. Although many think this pre-Renaissance period was one of "medieval" ignorance and backwardness, in truth, great progress had been made in the human condition during the 12th and early 13th centuries. The population of Europe rose from 58 million in 1100 to 79 million in 1250—an increase of 36 percent—with a concurrent, rapid increase in urbanization and the emergence of many new towns and cities. A great deal of new technology was brought on line, including the spread of power generation technologies, primarily waterwheels and windmills, and improvements in mining, agriculture, and shipbuilding. A significant factor in these advances was the importation of new inventions and techniques from China, as well as from the Arab world. It was precisely this progress in the human condition, this increased mastery over nature, which made the emergence of

Statue of Dante at Naples.

Dante, Giotto, and others possible.

Nevertheless, Europe was still a fragmented, intensely oligarchical society, and by the middle of the 13th Century, the upward curve of progress had been destroyed. In several of his writings, including the *Commedia*, Dante ties the worsening crisis in Italy to the emergence of a usurious money economy. Dante's particular emphasis was on the introduction of the gold Florin in 1252. It was the Florin that became the accounting currency for the private banking houses of Bardi, Peruzzi, Frescobaldi, and others, who proceeded to loot, bankrupt, and destroy the peoples of Europe in the late 13th and 14th centuries.

Venice, which had emerged as the *primus inter pares* among the Italian city-states following its conquest of Constantinople in 1204, led the way in this orgy of oligarchical looting, and the key destructive dynamic of this period was centered in the alliance of Venice, the Church, and the Norman (*Angevin*) monarchy of England, which ruled half of France. Dante reserves particular vitriol for the involvement of the Papacy and the Church hierarchy in the degeneracy, destruction, and financial looting he witnessed during his lifetime.

By the time that Dante was first elected to public office in 1295, Italy and most of Europe had become a speculators' paradise, dominated by Venice, the Lombard bankers, and a corrupt and venal Papacy. By 1290 the European population had begun to decline. Agricultural and wool production collapsed, food disappeared in many areas, and many smaller and medium-sized towns were abandoned. It was within this downward spiral that Dante waged his war. The economy and the society of Europe all came crashing down in the horrors of the 14th Century. But then, in the midst of unspeakable human suffering, at what seemed the nadir of human existence, the mind of Dante would resurface, and it would "light the path" for a way forward into a better future.

A Brief Initial Biography

Dante Alighieri came from a family of minor aristocracy. He grew up in the San Piero district of Florence. His mother died when he was ten; when his father died six years later, he came under the guardianship of Brunetto Latini, a Florentine aristocrat, a student of Cicero, and a leader of Florence after he became one of the six ruling Priors of Florence in 1287.

At that time, almost every city in northern Italy was gripped by ongoing warfare between the Guelph and Ghibelline parties. Generally, the Ghibellines were loyal to the Holy Roman Emperor, whose power lay primarily in Germany, and the Guelphs were partisans of the Pope, although in reality, it was the usury-centered Vatican-Venetian-Angevin alliance which defined the Guelph party. In practice, many of these political lines shifted over time and, in some cases, the party names came to have directly opposite meanings.

Warfare between the parties was bloody and went on for decades. In Florence, the Ghibellines were overthrown by the Guelphs in 1267,[1] and this was followed by the final military defeat of the Ghibellines in 1289,[2] after which the triumphant Guelph Party split into two mutually hostile factions, the [*Bianchi* (Whites) and the *Neri* (Blacks), the latter being the extreme, pro-Papal

---

1. Following Charles of Anjou's defeat of Manfred, the son of Frederick II Hohenstaufen, in 1266.
2. At the Battle of Campaldino, in which Dante participated as a cavalryman.

party. Dante, whose family was historically associated with the Guelph Party, joined the Whites in his adulthood.

In 1295, the conflict between the White and Black factions worsened, erupting in bloodshed. On November 1, 1301, a foreign army, backed by Pope Boniface and led by Charles of Valois, the son of the French king, occupied Florence. Under Charles' protection, the Blacks seized control of the government and carried out indiscriminate massacres of the Whites for seven days.

By this time Dante was the premier leader of the White Party in Florence and a dominant force in the Florentine government. He had been elected to the ruling Council of One Hundred early in 1295, and then to the more powerful Council of Thirty-Six later that same year. On June 15, 1300, Dante became one of the six ruling Priors. By 1301, he was the most important political leader. Boccaccio says that, by 1301, "nothing was done in Florence without Dante being consulted."

In the fall of 1301, Dante led a diplomatic mission to Rome to meet the Pope. It was a time of great crisis, and Dante knew he was needed in both Florence and Rome. Boccaccio reports him as saying, "If I go, who stays? If I stay, who goes?" When Charles's army occupied Florence and the massacres began, the Pope allowed all of the other members of the delegation to return home, but he ordered Dante alone to remain in Rome. In January 1302, *in absentia*, Dante was officially charged with bribery, trafficking in offices, and other crimes by the Black Guelph authorities. He was fined, banished for two years, and permanently excluded from office. Two months later, the Florentine government condemned Dante to be burnt to death if he re-entered the city or fell into the hands of Florentine authorities.[3] Dante never returned to Florence.

II. Shaping Poetic Creativity

In 1283, at the age of seventeen, Dante wrote the poem *A ciascun'alma presa*. It was a modest sonnet, but it brought him to the attention of Guido Cavalcanti, leader of the *dolce stil nuovo* (sweet new style)[4] poetry movement, a group of *fedeli d'amour* (faithful followers of love). This group of mostly upper-class young

men were heavily influenced by the earlier (roughly 1150-1225) efforts of the troubadour movement, a networks of poets centered in the *langue d'oc* region of southern France and northern Spain. The troubadours, whose work was dominated by themes of chivalrous love, are noteworthy both for the lyric quality of their poetry (actually songs) and for the fact that almost all of their works were composed in the *Occitan* vernacular of the region.

The second great influence on the Florentine poets was the Sicilian School, which flourished in the mid-13th Century under the sponsorship of Frederick II Hohenstaufen. Frederick's life was a grand effort to dismantle the feudal system of social organization inherited from the Normans, and as he eradicated fiefdoms throughout his realm, his poets developed a new poetic language based on a mixture of local vernaculars with a richness of vocabulary—what is known as a *koiné* language. It was in Sicily that the modern sonnet form was invented and where the *canzone* was developed. The other striking feature of Sicilian poetry is the introduction of a kinder, gentler type of woman than that found in the French model. Dante was greatly influenced by the Sicilian School, and he quotes widely from it in his studies, especially in *De Vulgari Eloquentia*.

For roughly a decade, from 1283 to 1293, Dante honed his poetic skills. He composed many sonnets, a number of which were later incorporated into *La Vita Nuova*. It was also during this time that, according to Boccaccio, Dante engaged in an intensive study of both Boethius and Cicero.

Dante's "mentor" during this period was Guido Cavalcanti, who would later become a prominent leader of the White Guelphs. Dante also singles out both Bonagiunta Orbicciani and Guido Guinizzelli as primary influences on his poetic development. In Canto XXVI of "Purgatorio," in the *Commedia*, Dante describes himself as a disciple of Guinizzelli.[5]

All of this work culminated in the publication in 1293 or 1294 of *La Vita Nuova*.

La Vita Nuova

Although still far removed from the transcendent glory of the *Commedia*, *La Vita Nuova* already pro-

---

3. The death sentence against Dante was finally rescinded by the Florentine government in 2008.

4. It was Dante, himself, who gave this name to the Florentine group.

5. Despite Dante's respect for, and acknowledged debt to many of his colleagues of the *Dolce Stil Nuovo*, in his *Commedia* he does not place any of them in the *Paradiso*, although Bonagiunta Orbicciani does manage to make it into the sixth terrace (Gluttony) of the *Purgatorio*.

claimed the opening salvo of a new culture for human society. Dante's subject is Beatrice, with whom he "fell in love" at the age of nine, and the book's underlying story extends over sixteen years until Beatrice's death in 1290. But *La Vita Nuova* is not a tragic romance.[6] Already, Dante has made a sharp break with the love poetry of the French model. In Dante, love is based on reason, not appetites. Derived from Dante's self-identified "book of memory," *La Vita Nuova* chronicles Dante's struggle for intellectual and moral growth, and this struggle is not merely personal and existential—and certainly not sensual—but rises to higher insights into the culture and human condition of Florence.

What most shocked his contemporaries was that the entire work is composed in the Florentine vernacular. *La Vita Nuova* is a sequence of sonnets interspersed with

prose.[7] The lyrics of the troubadours and the works of the Sicilian School all represented what one might call court poetry, written for a very limited, elite audience, but Dante's purpose was not to titillate or amuse an aristocratic class. At that time it was unheard of that a serious author would compose *prose* in the vernacular. In essence, in *La Vita Nuova*, Dante has already announced his intention, not simply to write beautiful poems, but to develop a new language for the advancement of human culture, for the unleashing of hitherto dormant cognitive and creative potential. His work was intended for everyone.

III. The Vernacular

Dante authored two works that explicitly, and in depth, take up the issue of the vernacular, *De Vulgari Eloquentia* and *Convivio*. Boccaccio dates the writing of *De Vulgari Eloquentia* to 1318, but there is compel-

---

6. The reputation of *La Vita Nuova* as a "romantic" work is largely due to the influence of the 19th Century proto-fascist Dante Gabriel Rossetti.

7. *La Vita Nuova* is the only work by Dante in which most of the poetry is in sonnet form and written in iambic pentameter.

Ripples through Time

The power of the human soul reaches out over centuries. In the case of Alessandro Manzoni and his masterpiece *I Promessi Sposi* (The Betrothed), that striving for human salvation burst forth once again. Considered the greatest novel in the Italian language, *I Promessi Sposi* was first published in 1827. But Manzoni was not happy with the final outcome, and he rewrote it in the Florentine dialect of Dante, publishing a new version in 1842 to universal acclaim. As Manzoni said in one of his final letters, his novel did not reach its full potential until it had undergone a "rinsing in the Arno."

The protagonists of the story are the betrothed couple Lucia and Renzo, and it is set in and around Milan at the time of the great plague of 1630, when Italy was being ravaged by foreign troops and famine. Manzoni, himself, lived at a time of great crisis, of the *Risorgimento* and the struggle of Italy to free itself from foreign oppression. Manzoni's story of the two lovers is really the story of Italy, and his

theme of *agapic* redemption reverberated throughout the nation.

Giuseppe Verdi stood in awe of Manzoni. In 1867, he wrote that *I Promessi Sposi* was "one of the greatest [books] to emerge from the human mind" and "not only a book, but a consolation for humanity." After his first meeting with Manzoni, Verdi wrote to a friend, "I would have gone down on my knees before him if we were allowed to worship men. They say it is wrong to do so, and it may be, although we raise up on altars many that have neither the talent nor the virtue of Manzoni and indeed are perfect scoundrels." On the first anniversary of Manzoni's death Verdi premiered his *Requiem*, a work which became known at that time as "Manzoni's Requiem."

Manzoni championed the Florentine vernacular throughout his lifetime, leading an eventually successful fight for the adoption of Dante's vernacular as the national language of the unified Italian nation. He stated that Dante was striving "to create a form worthy of representing the national idea," and in 1868 he published a famous letter on the subject of *De Vulgari Eloquentia*.

ling historical evidence to show that at least the first of that work's two books was written earlier, 1303-1304, while Dante was in Verona. The *Convivio* was probably written between 1305 and 1307.

De Vulgari Eloquentia is diabolical. It is the only one of his major works that he wrote in Latin; yet the entire argument of the work is to prove not only the worth but the superiority of the vernacular over Latin as a means of poetic, scientific, and philosophical expression. Dante insisted on the necessity to invent, and expand the power of, a new language. He fiercely defended this idea throughout his life.

For example, between 1319 and 1321, toward the end of Dante's life, there was a concerted effort by Giovanni del Virgilio—an associate of the prominent Paduan scholar and champion of classical Latin, Albertino Mussato—to induce Dante to abandon the vernacular as "unworthy" of his literary talents. Del Virgilio offered Dante the prospect of being named the poet laureate of Bologna if he would rewrite *Inferno* from the "lowly" vernacular into Latin, saying, "recast the great poem in Latin and the laurel may be yours." In response, Dante sent him ten cantos of the "Paradiso" in Italian, upon which he was then working, stating that with the completion of the "Paradiso," he hoped instead to receive the laureate crown in Florence.

Dante was under constant, almost universal, attack for his use of the vernacular, but he never wavered. He returned to the subject again and again: Major sections of the *Vita Nuova*, the *Convivio*, the *Commedia* are given over to this purpose, not to mention the entirety of *De Vulgari Eloquentia*. In the *Commedia*, where Dante has Virgil recite a poem in Latin, Dante responds in Italian, and the disappearance of Virgil prior to the entrance into Paradise—where only the vernacular is uttered—drives the point home.

In exploring and expanding the many potentials of the vernacular, particularly in the *Convivio*, Dante uses this discussion of language to examine his own creative process. He transforms the vernacular into a vehicle for intellectual thought—science and poetry. In so doing, he creates the modern Italian language, and he improves, expands, and tests the limits of that language. He offers an invitation and a means whereby every Italian might be uplifted and have access to the higher, more subtle powers of mind.

De Vulgari Eloquentia is a rigorous, and vigorous, defense of the vernacular and is, essentially, a system-

"Paradiso," Canto XXXI. Illustration from the series by Gustave Doré.

atic argument for what the basis for that language must be. He examines the three regional dialects of *oc* (southern France, Catalonia), *oïl* (northern France) and *sì* (Italy); then he turns to the specifics of fourteen different Italian dialects. He argues for a single *volgare* which should include all the best features of each dialect, but he settles on the Florentine version of Tuscan as the basis from which the national language must develop. This is precisely what happened in the years following Dante's death, as the *Commedia* became the basis for a new Italian language culture.

In declaring his faith and his love for the vernacular in the *Convivio*, Dante writes:

"This shall be the new light, the new Sun, which shall rise when the worn-out one shall set, and shall give light to them who are in shadow and in darkness because of the old Sun, which does not enlighten them."

The *Convivio*

The *Convivio* is divided into four books, the first of which is given over to an advanced argument in favor of the vernacular. Each of the remaining books is introduced by a long beautiful *canzone*. Book Two begins with the *canzone*, *"Voi che intendendo il terzo ciel movete"* (You who move the third heaven with an act of the intellect) and Book Three begins with, *"Amor che ne la mente mi ragiona"* (Love, who speaks to me within my mind). It must be remembered that *canzoni* are songs, and the original *canzoni* of the troubadours and trouvères were sung.

In speaking of the vernacular in Book One, Dante says,

> Now perfect generosity may be noted in three characteristics of the vernacular which would not have been consequential in the use of Latin. The first is that of giving to many people; the second is that of giving things of use; the third is that of giving without being asked.
>
> To give to and assist one person is good, but perfect goodness is to give to and assist many in that this resembles the beneficence of God, who is the universal benefactor.
>
> Latin would have failed to meet all of the three conditions mentioned above, all of which must be met for a gift to display complete generosity . . .

and,

> I say that innate love moves the lover to do three things above all: firstly to enhance the beloved object; secondly to be solicitous on its behalf; and thirdly to defend it, which happens continually as anyone can observe. These three motives made me adopt the vernacular, which I love and have loved both innately and contingently.

and,

> All these groups taken together [i.e., those who oppose the vernacular] comprise the vile Italian wretches who despise this rich vernacular, which, if it is base in any way, is base only insofar as it issues from the meretricious lips of these adulterers, by whom the blind are led.

Books Two and Three both begin with long poems (songs) which are addressed to *Lady Philosophy*, and these poems are both followed by lengthy prose sections, wherein Dante examines the workings of his own mind, his own sense of identity, the nature of the universe— and throughout all of it, he is testing the limits of, expanding the subtleties of, and developing the power of his new language. His discussion of the language and lyrics within each of the *canzoni* is crucial to this.

To grasp a sense of this, consider the following excerpt from Chapter 15 of Book Two:

> From the analogies discussed above, it is obvious who those movers are whom I address: They are the movers of that heaven, such as Boethius and Cicero, who guided me by the sweetness of their discourse along the path of love, that is in pursuit of the most gentle lady Philosophy, with the rays of their star, that is their writings of her; because the written word is in every science a star filled with light that reveals that science. Understanding this, we can then perceive the true meaning of the first stanza of the *canzone* before us, by way of the literal meaning. By means of that exposition, the second stanza may also be adequately addressed, as far as: One that makes me look upon a lady.
>
> Let us observe here that this lady is Philosophy, truly a lady full of sweetness, adorned with honor, marvelous in wisdom, glorious in freedom, as will be shown in the third book, which will treat of her nobility. And when I say: Who wishes to see bliss, let his eyes on this lady gaze, then this lady's eyes are her proofs by reason, which directed into the eyes of the intellect, enamour the soul freed from confusion. Oh sweet and ineffable look, captivating the human mind, that appears in the eyes of Philosophy when she speaks with her lovers! Truly salvation lies in you, so that he who gazes on you is blessed and saved from the deathliness of vice and ignorance.

and, from Chapter 3, Book Three:

> Then, since this highest nature is called mind, as explained above, I say in the *canzone* that: "Love speaks within my mind," to make it clear that it is the love that springs from the noblest nature of truth and virtue, and to counter any false opinion regarding myself that my love was aimed at sensual delight . . .
>
> Such is the first ineffable aspect of what I take for them in the *canzone*; and then I speak of the other when I say: "Love's speech." I say that my thought, that is Love's word, sounds in me so sweetly that my soul, that is my affection, is on fire to speak it with my tongue; and because I cannot, I write that the soul therefore laments,

saying: "Alas, that I lack power." This is the second ineffable aspect of my theme: that is, that the tongue cannot reproduce completely what the intellect perceives. And I also say: "My soul which feels and hears him"; that is hears the words, and feels the sweetness of the sound.

Book Four of the *Convivio*[8] is given over to a discussion of true human nobility—as opposed to the "nobility" of the hereditary oligarchical aristocracy. Dante attacks the question of what defines a truly noble character; he defines that nobility as a process of increasing perfection within the human individual. Again, the book is introduced by a beautiful *canzone*: *"Le dolci rime d'amor"* (Those sweet poems of love).

The *Convivio* is a prodigious, challenging work. I could say much more, but will leave it to the initiative of the reader to pursue its wonders further. In the *Convivio*, Dante is teaching people how to read; he is teaching people how to think; he is teaching a new language; and he is creating a new audience for a new civilization. He is inviting *you* to the *Banquet*, and it is your decision whether to participate or not.

IV. War with the Oligarchy

After his banishment from Florence, Dante devoted himself for the next three years, from 1301 to 1304, to creating and then leading a new alliance between the White Guelphs and the Ghibellines. He traveled from city to city, with no permanent residence, except for an extended stay in Verona. He recruited, he advised, and he organized. This initiative came to a conclusion on July 19, 1304, when a Ghibelline-White military force, intent on recapturing Florence, suffered a disastrous defeat at La Lastra, outside the city walls of Florence.

Following this, Dante met with leaders of the Whites, on July 30 in Arezzo, advised them on a future course of action, and then left. He spent the next year traveling alone. He had become "a party unto [him] self."

He traveled to Bologna, then to Treviso, and finally to Padua, where he remained for some time, meeting

Giotto, conversing with him for several months, and studying his frescos at the Scrovegni Chapel.

During this time, a new Pope was elected, Clement V. Clement would prove a far deadlier opponent than Boniface, and it was Clement, in alliance with the French King Philip IV, who moved the Papacy to Avignon in 1305, where it remained for seventy-three years.[9]

Between 1306 and 1309 Dante was in Lucca, Lunigiana, Casentino, and then back in Lucca. It was during this time that he wrote the *Convivio* and possibly began work on the "Inferno."[10] In the *Convivio* Dante describes the circumstances of his life at that time, "I have gone about as a beggar, showing against my will the wound of fortune. . . . Verily I have been a ship without sails and without rudder, driven to various harbors and shores by the parching wind which blows from pinching poverty."

Henry VII

On January 6, 1309, Henry of Luxembourg is crowned as Holy Roman Emperor at Aachen. He immediately announces his intention to reassert traditional and legal authority over the cities of northern Italy. In November 1310, Henry's army enters Turin.

Dante rushes to his side and travels with the army from Turin to Asti, and then to Vercelli and Milan. He begins writing a series of open letters (*Epistole*) rallying support for Henry's cause. The first of these, directed to the leaders of Florence, *"Ecce nune tempus acceptabile,"* declares the moral responsibility of Florence to submit to the Emperor. When Florence refuses, Dante writes a second *Epistola* denouncing them.

On January 6, 1311, Henry enters Milan, where he is crowned King of Italy. Dante attends the coronation and meets Henry. For the next two years, Henry's cause becomes Dante's cause. In March and April, he

---

8. Dante intended a work of fifteen books, with fourteen *canzone*, but the *Convivio* was incomplete at the time of his death.

9. Dante places all of these—Boniface, Clement, and Philip—in the *Inferno*, and the very last words which Dante has Beatrice speak in the "Paradiso" are a fierce denunciation of Clement. Avignon, in southern France, was within the hereditary realm of the House of Anjou, and Clement, who was not Italian, was born and raised in Aquitaine.

10. The dating of the *Commedia* is a matter of controversy. Some claim that Dante began writing the "Inferno" as early as 1304. Others strongly disagree. What is known with certainty is that copies of both the "Inferno" and the "Purgatorio" were circulating by 1314-1315. It is also established that Dante had begun writing the "Paradiso" by 1316, and that it was completed in late 1320 or early 1321.

writes two *Epistole* urging Henry to take Florence by force and to seize "the most wicked Florentines within." He also condemns Clement V for both simony and political treachery. In December, Henry issues a proclamation placing Florence under the ban of the Holy Roman Empire, and declaring the Florentine exiles—including Dante—under his special protection.

Henry's army proceeds to Brescia, Genoa, and Vicenza. By April of 1312, Henry is at Pisa, with Dante by his side. Henry then directs his army toward Rome. After fierce fighting, his army enters the City on May 7, 1312. At this point, King Robert of Naples, the brother of Charles of Anjou, enters the war against the Emperor. For his service to the Papal cause, Robert would later be named a Senator of Rome, and Vicar General of all Italy, and it was Robert's army which fought Henry's forces throughout 1312 and 1313.[11]

In September of 1312, Henry's army attacks Florence and quickly defeats the defending army, forcing it back within the walls of the city. After a six week siege and a series of attacks on the defenses, Henry recognizes that he does not have a sufficient force to take the city by force, and withdraws. He subdues the rest of Tuscany and occupies Lucca. At this point, he prepares for a full assault on Naples. He begins building a fleet for a naval attack, and his army moves south. His first target is Siena, to which he lays siege. But it is here, in the midst of the siege, that Henry dies, of malaria, on August 24, 1313.[12]

Dante Alighieri, in fresco by Andrea del Castagno, kept in the Uffizi in Florence.

A Beacon that Refuses to be Extinguished

With the sudden death of Henry, the imperial cause disintegrated in Italy, and Henry's armies disbanded or returned to northern Europe. Of Dante's fate, little is known for the next two years. As one biographer states, during this time, "his steps are lost in darkness." All hope of his returning to Florence had vanished. It is known that he lived, briefly, in Lucca, under the protection of the Ghibelline leader Uguccione della Faggiuola. There are also indications that he was working on the "Purgatorio" during this time.

By this time Dante was seen—by both enemies and friends—as the beacon of resistance against the Angevin monstrosity. The mere mention of his name evoked terror and self-befoulment among the oligarchical elite. In November of 1315, the Angevin vicar in Tuscany, Baldo d'Aguglione, condemned Dante and his sons to death by beheading, and when a sweeping general amnesty was declared in Florence, in 1316, for all of the White Guelph and Ghibelline opponents of the Angevin regime, Dante, alone, was excluded.

Among his friends and allies, Dante was viewed as the spokesman for *all* of Italy. Many had supported the campaigns of Emperor Henry, but it was Dante who was their voice. And it was not a pragmatic voice, but one imbued with the vision of *De Vulgari Eloquentia*, the *Convivio*, his *Epistole*, and the opening cantos of his *Commedia*, which were by then beginning to circulate. Dante was defining a higher-ordered future for all of Italy, nay, for all of humanity. And this was recognized by many.

In 1315 Dante was invited to Verona by the great Ghibelline leader, Cangrande della Scala. He would reside there for three years. It was during his time in Verona that Dante wrote *De Monarchia* and began work on the "Paradiso."

Cangrande was a great and remarkable individual, named by Henry VII as "Vicar to the Emperor." As a

---

11. In addition to ruling the Kingdom of Naples, the Angevin Robert was also the Sovereign of the so-called Kingdom of Arles, within which Avignon—and the residence of Pope Clement—was located.

12. Dante places Henry in the "Paradiso" (Canto XXX). Since the *Commedia* is set in the year 1300, when Henry was still alive, Dante creates an *alto Arrigo* to hold the place of honor for Henry, of whom Dante says, "He who came to reform Italy before she was ready for it."

general, he led his troops into battle numerous times for more than thirty years. He was, as well, a fervent sponsor of the arts and learning.[13] The years 1315-1318 witnessed numerous military victories of the Ghibelline leaders Cangrande and Uguccione della Faggiuola against the forces of Robert of Anjou, and while they had no hope of overthrowing the Angevin power, they nevertheless succeeded in maintaining and expanding the Ghibelline strongholds.

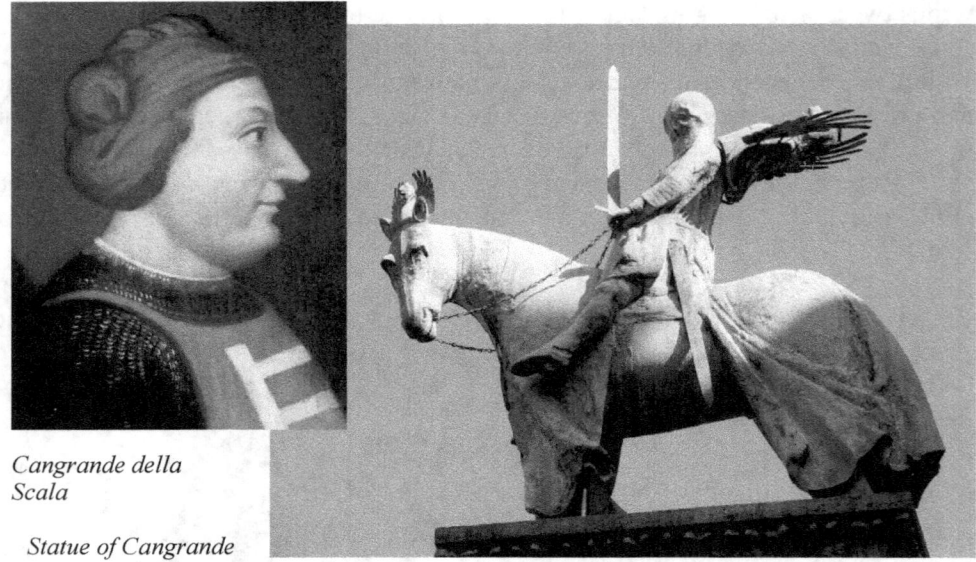

Cangrande della Scala

Statue of Cangrande in Verona.

Dante's attitude toward Cangrande was explicit. Not only does he say of him in the "Paradiso," "even his enemies would be unable to keep silent about him," but in 1316 he issued his *Epistola* No. 13, dedicating the entire "Paradiso" to Cangrande.

By September 1316, all hope for a reform and purification of the Church were dashed with the election of a new Pope, John XXII. A Frenchman from Cahors, John would keep the Papal See at Avignon, and it was during his lengthy reign that the Papacy became massively involved in the financial and economic looting of Europe and the city of Avignon became a center of trans-Alpine banking. In "Inferno" Canto XI, Dante places John XXII's own home city of Cahors alongside Sodom and declares them synonymous with sin.

De Monarchia

Ignorant commentators often define *De Monarchia* as a simple defense of imperial rule over the cities and provinces of Italy, or even as a paean to the glorious heritage of the Roman Empire. It is far, far more than that. Dante defines his purpose very clearly in his introduction:

> All men on whom the Higher Nature has stamped the love of truth should especially concern themselves in laboring for posterity, in order that

future generations may be enriched by their efforts, as they themselves were made rich by the efforts of generations past. For that man who is imbued with public teachings, but cares not to contribute something to the public good, is far in arrears of his duty, let him be assured; he is, indeed, not "a tree planted by the rivers of water that bringeth forth his fruit in his season," but rather a destructive whirlpool, always engulfing, and never giving back what it has devoured. Often meditating with myself upon these things, lest I should some day be found guilty of the charge of the buried talent, I desire for the public weal, not only to burgeon, but to bear fruit, and to establish truths unattempted by others.

He drives the point home with the title of Chapter II: "To What End Does Government Exist Among All Men?"

It is impossible here to explore in depth the full richness of *Monarchia*, and once again the only course of action available to the reader is to plunge into it for one's self. There is no substitute for reading this work in its entirety. Cliff's Notes will not do.

Much is made by dilettantes of Dante's adherence to the imperial cause against the alleged—but actually non-existent—"republican" nature of the Italian city-states, as well as to Dante's lengthy and positive discussion of the character of imperial Rome, but the deeper issues raised by Dante are often missed. What he is

---

13. It was also during his time in Verona that Dante renewed his acquaintance with Giotto, who was brought to the city by Cangrande to create a series of frescos.

posing is the question of universal principles which must govern the functioning of human society and become the basis for the individual human identity.

In Chapter II, he states:

> As every truth which is not a first principle is manifested by the truth of some first principle, it is necessary in every investigation to know the first principle to which we may return, in analysis, for the proof of all propositions which are subsequently assumed. And as the present treatise is an investigation, we must before all else search out a basic principle, on the validity of which will depend whatever follows.
>
> Since the matter under consideration is governmental, nay, is the very source and first principle of right governments, and since everything governmental is subject to our control, it is clear that our present theme is primarily adapted for action rather than for speculation.
>
> So if there exists an end for universal government among men, that end will be the basic principle through which all things to be proved hereafter may be demonstrated satisfactorily. But to believe that there is an end for this government and for that government, and that there is no single end common to all, would indeed be irrational.

And he says in Chapter IV:

> It has thus been sufficiently set forth that the proper work of the human race, taken as a whole, is to set in action the whole capacity of that understanding which is capable of development: first in the way of speculation, and then, by its extension, in the way of action.

Throughout the entirety of the work there are repeated references to the Roman Republic and to the "sacred example" of Cincinnatus,[14] and it becomes very clear that Dante's true subject is the moral basis for a citizenry, not the specific form of government. There is

---

14. The example of Cincinnatus is featured again, two centuries later, in Machiavelli's *Discourses on the First Ten Books of Titus Livius*. Machiavelli was an avid student of Dante, and borrowings from the *Commedia* are found in his letters and a number of his works. The influence of Dante's lyrics is also very apparent in Machiavelli's neglected but beautiful poetry.

an extensive investigation into the subject of Free Will, wherein Dante states that animals do not possess free will because they are governed by appetites, but man is free to develop his goodness, his intellectual powers, and the society within which he lives—that, in this manner alone, is man truly free. In Chapter XII, he says:

> It is therefore again manifest that this liberty, or this principle of all our liberty, is the greatest gift bestowed by God on mankind: by it alone we gain happiness as men: by it alone we gain happiness elsewhere as gods. But if this is so, who will say that humankind is not in its best state, when it can most use this principle?

Thus Dante is posing not merely the *form* of society or the mechanics of government, but the question of the *nature* of human identity required for the advancement of the human species.

This question of the universal divine nature of the human identity, which permeates both the *minimum* of the human individual and the *maximum* of society as a whole, is raised explicitly in Book Three of the *Monarchia*, "Whether the Authority of the Roman Monarch Derives from God Immediately or From Some Vicar of God." On the surface, the subject is the centuries old conflict between the Pope and the Emperor and the assertion by the Guelph Party that the Emperor is subservient to the Pope. Dante, obviously, opposes that claim, but he takes his argument to a far more profound level.

Under the existing order of things in Dante's time, kings, princes, lords, and doges were able to impose whatever arbitrary authority they chose, and their whims were *de facto* law, so long as the Pope did not intervene. Dante argues that all civilian authority must flow from a natural, inherent relationship with Divine Law, one to be found in the imperishable nature of the human soul. Rulers were not bound or controlled by the dictates of Popes; neither were they free to do as they chose. Only a government which is faithful to a true mission for the development of the citizenry is legitimate.

De Monarchia was a declaration of war—a flanking attack on the highest epistemological level—against the Angevin-Papal-Usury power, and Dante's enemies reacted accordingly with denunciations and threats. It was written in 1317 or 1318, at the same time that Dante had begun work on the "Paradiso." That reality alone suffices to demolish all notions that, after the death of Henry VII, Dante "abandoned" politics and turned more fully to theological pursuits. Shortly after Dante's death, a Dominican monk from Rimini, Fra Guido Vernani, published *De Reprobatione Monarchie Composita a Dante*, declaring Dante's works as a danger to the Faith and denouncing *De Monarchia* as a book of cruel and pestilent poison. In 1329 the Guelph leaders of Bologna publicly burned all of the copies of *De Monarchia* that they were able to locate and seize.

Final Journey

In late 1317, Dante left Verona and once again became a "man without a city," traveling in the Romagna. As Boccaccio puts it, Dante "departed to Romagna, where his last day, that was to put an end to all his toils, awaited him." Most of the region's cities were Black Guelph strongholds. Bologna was fiercely loyal to Robert of Anjou, as were

At the court of Guido Novello.

Forli, Rimini, Fano, and Cesena. Ferrara, which had been occupied by French troops, was liberated by the Marquis d'Este in 1317, amidst horrendous bloodshed, and the cities of Faenza and Imola were the scenes of ongoing warfare and widespread death as the Papal and Imperial parties struggled for supremacy.

Nothing is known of Dante's movements in those months as he traversed the treacherous landscape, but he was finally rescued from this danger in January 1318, when he received an invitation from the ruler of Ravenna, Guido Novello da Polenta, to take refuge in his city. He was joined there by three of his children. As Boccaccio reports:

> When it came to his [de Polenta's] ears, that Dante, beyond all expectation, was now in Romagna and in such desperate plight, he, who had long time before known his worth by fame, resolved to receive him and do him honor. Nor did he wait to be requested by him to do this, but considering with how great shame men of worth request such favors, with liberal mind and with free proffers, he approached him, requesting from Dante of special grace that which he knew Dante must needs have begged of him, to wit, that it might please him to abide with him.

From Ravenna issued forth the glory of the "Paradiso." As he completed individual cantos, Dante sent them to Cangrande della Scala at Verona, perhaps the most precious gifts in all of human history that one friend has sent to another. Boccaccio writes that Dante held della Scala "in reverence above all other men," and that della Scala, "when he had seen them, he copied them for whoso desired them." Thus, do the names Guido Novello da Polenta and Cangrande della Scala shine forth, to this day, as beacons of what earthly leaders can aspire to be, in making the realization of the "Paradiso" possible.

In the summer of 1321 the Venetian Empire prepared a war of annihilation against Ravenna, with the intention of exterminating the family of Guido Novello and annexing Ravenna to Venetian territory. The Doge of Venice, Giovanni Soranzo, entered into an alliance with Forli, and preparations were made for a military offensive. At the request of Guido Novello da Polenta, Dante accepted a mission to lead a delegation to Venice for the purpose of negotiating a peace agreement. The Venetian authorities refused to meet with Dante, despite repeated attempts. During his stay in Venice, Dante became seriously ill, and when he requested sea passage back to Ravenna, he was refused. Together with his party, the feverish Dante was forced to return to Ravenna via an arduous land route. He arrived in Ravenna on September 12, 1321, and after two days of worsening sickness, he died. He was buried, in Ravenna, at the church of San Pier Maggiore, where he remains, rightly, to this day.

Over the centuries, the rulers of Florence have made repeated attempts to "take back" the one they had once persecuted and rejected. In 1519 the Medici Pope Leo X ordered that Dante's bones be transferred from Ravenna to Florence, but the papal order was refused. Instead, an empty coffin was sent back, and the Franciscan monks who had charge of Dante's remains removed them from the tomb, and buried them secretly in the Franciscan monastery in Sienzo. In 1810, the same order of monks moved the bones once again to hide the remains of Dante from the armed forces of Napoleon Bonaparte. Finally, in 1865 Dante's remains were returned to San Pier Maggiore (now the Basilica of Saint Francis) and a small tomb was built to hold them.

In 1829 the city of Florence erected an ornate tomb for Dante in the Basilica of Santa Croce. The inscription on the tomb reads, "Honor the most exalted poet," but unfortunately for Florence, the tomb stands empty to this day. Dante is not there. The judgement on Florence is best given by Boccaccio:

> In place of reward, he suffered an unjust and hasty sentence, perpetual banishment, the alienation of his family estate, and, if that could have been accomplished, the staining of his glorious fame by false accusations. To this the fresh traces of his flight, his bones buried in another country, his children scattered in others' houses, still in part bear witness. If all the other iniquities of Florence could be concealed from the all-seeing eyes of God, would not this alone suffice to draw down upon her His wrath? Yea, verily.

V. Victory

References to Dante, quotations from Dante, and the soul of Dante all flow through the works of Giovanni Boccaccio, as the singular idea is inseparable from the whole. His earliest letters reveal the influence of Dante, and his first major work written at the age of twenty-three, *Filocolo*, shows the influence of the *Vita Nuova*. In *Amorosa Visione* he calls Dante the "lord of all knowledge,"[15] and his musical *ballate* in the *Decam-*

Tomb of Dante Alighieri in Ravenna.

eron are modeled on the lyrics of Dante.

Boccaccio knew intimately Dante's nephew Andrea Poggi, and it was from him that Boccaccio received much information about Dante. He knew, as well, Dino Perini, a close friend of Dante, and during his two visits to Ravenna, in 1346 and 1353, he met and conversed both with Dante's daughter, Antonia (who later became a nun, taking the name Sister Beatrice), and Piero Giardino, one of Dante's most devoted friends. It was from these sources, as well as others, that Boccaccio would publish, in 1357, his *Vita di Dante* (Life of Dante), also known as *Trattatello in Laude di Dante* (Little Tractate in Praise of Dante).[16]

In August 1373, Boccaccio received a commission from the Priors of the Guilds and the Standard-Bearer of Justice to give a year of public lectures on Dante's *Commedia*. The lectures began on Sunday, October 23, in the church of Santo Stefano in Badia, Florence. These were *daily* lectures, totaling about one hundred

---

15. The poem *Amorosa Visione*, directly modeled on the *Commedia*, contains 50 Cantos in *terza rima*. In the poem, both Dante and Giotto are celebrated, by name, as standing above all other artists, ancient or modern.

16. Available here.

and lasting for almost four months, until Boccaccio was forced to withdraw due to illness. In attendance were many who were then working on the construction of the Duomo, so as work proceeded on the Cathedral, the mind of Dante was there to guide them.

With Boccaccio, Dante's lifelong mission on behalf of the *illustrious vernacular* triumphed. It is true that in 15th Century Italy, many "Renaissance scholars" attempted to force a return to classical Latin as the only "accepted" medium for transmitting philosophical and literary ideas, but a product of human creativity, once recognized and socialized, can never be eradicated. This is the true secret of the relationship between Boccaccio and Petrarch. Often, the elder Petrarch is described as the polished mentor to the younger, less erudite Boccaccio, but in reality, the relationship was vice versa. It was Boccaccio, who for decades, battled unyieldingly with the classical Latinist Petrarch on the subject of the vernacular, and there are many letters still extant to attest to this. It was Boccaccio who represented the future.

Geoffrey Chaucer made several visits to Italy, including one in 1372, one year prior to Boccaccio's lectures at Santo Stefano. Chaucer called Dante "the grete poete of Itaille." He expressed great admiration for the *Commedia* to friends, and he attempted to use Dante's rhyming verse stanza form, the *terza rima*, in a number of locations. But it was to Boccaccio that Chaucer owed the greatest debt. "The Knight's Tale" from the *Canterbury Tales* is derived directly from Boccaccio's epic poem *Teseide*, and Boccaccio's *Il Filostrato* is the source for Chaucer's *Troilus and Criseyde*, as is Shakespeare's *Troilus and Cressida*. Many other works by Chaucer show the influence of the *Decameron*.

After Chaucer returned from his first Italian trip, there was a great change in his writing: a new boldness and richness—an expansion of the vocabulary, the invention of new words, and a stretching of the potential of the language. He also began to experiment more with meter, rhyme, and the poetic structure.[17] There is a new confidence. This is all seen in *The Canterbury Tales*. A modern language is being created. From Chaucer, the ultimate development of the poetic beauty and power of the English language would then only await the arrival of William Shakespeare.

Giovanni Boccaccio

The Renaissance Begins

Following Dante's death in 1321, at a time when the death penalty was still in effect against him in Florence, and following the publication of the *Commedia*, where many Popes, Black Guelphs, usurers, and Angevin leaders were condemned by name to the torments of the *Inferno*, it was not Boccaccio who first rose in Florence to proclaim Dante's greatness. That honor belongs to Giotto di Bondone. In 1337, during the last year of life, Giotto painted his final work, a fresco of Biblical scenes. It is located in the Podestà Chapel of the Palazzo del Bargello, Florence, and in it, Giotto depicts Dante, dressed in red, very prominently among those in Paradise. Giotto thereby conferred a kind of informal sainthood on Dante, less than 20 years after his death.

Giotto and Dante had conversed and worked together in Padua in 1305 and later renewed their acquaintance in Verona. Dante acknowledged the greatness of his living contemporary in "Purgatorio," Canto XI, when he has one of the characters say, "Cimabue believed that he held the field / In painting, and now Giotto has the cry, / So the fame of the former is obscure."

Anyone who has grappled with Dante, and who at the same time has studied the paintings of Giotto, is struck—as if by a thunderbolt—with the singularity of vision with which both men are imbued. Even the artistic illiterate, upon first viewing a Giotto fresco and com-

---

17. For example, his Rhyme Royal, a seven-line poetic structure in iambic pentameter.

A detail of Giotto's Bargello fresco. Dante is in the center in red cape.

Giotto di Bondone

paring it with the earlier Byzantine ikons, is often heard to say, "the people are so much more lifelike in Giotto." Yes, they are lifelike, and yes there is the use of perspective, but there is also an introspection, a deepness of character, a cognitive "soul" within the depicted individual that jumps out at the viewer. Giotto was saying something about the human identity, the human condition, and his efforts are coherent with Dante's fight for the vernacular, and with what Dante discloses in the *Commedia*.

In the final years of his life, Giotto became very close to the young Boccaccio.

Il Duomo

Il Duomo di Firenze—the Cathedral of Santa Maria del Fiore, in Florence—was begun in 1296. Originally intended to be built in the Gothic style, work on the Cathedral proceeded slowly, in fits and starts, for more than thirty years. Then, in 1331, the *Arte della Lana*, the guild of wool merchants, took over patronage of the cathedral construction. In 1334 they appointed Giotto to oversee the work. Giotto was to die in 1337, and during those three years, his major accomplishment was the building of the *campanile* (bell tower), which was com-

pleted after his death with a few significant changes in his design. His associate, Andrea Pisano, continued the work, but then all construction was halted due to the Black Death in 1348.

In 1348, between 75,000 and 100,000 residents of Florence died, perhaps as much as three-quarters of the city's population. No modern audience can even begin to appreciate the horror, fear, and mass psychosis of such a social breakdown. Alessandro Manzoni's rendering of the 1630 plague in Milan is terrifying, yet the 17th Century plague was limited in its effect when compared with the events of Boccaccio's time. Mass graves, thousands of unburied bodies, the disintegration of families, the surrender to hysteria—all of this became reality.

I cannot provide here an in-depth account of the economic policies of the 14th Century, but it must be stated, that the onset of the plague that swept Europe came at the end-point of a century of economic looting, largely carried out by the military, financial, and church forces to be found among Dante's enemies. The generally ignored, paramount role of Venice, the policies of the Black Guelph banking houses of Florence and the Lombard cities, the avarice of the Avignon papacy, and

Basilica di Santa Maria del Fiore in Florence.

back from the horror of the plague, was to restart construction on the Cathedral. Work resumed under the direction of Francesco Talenti, who enlarged its structure by redesigning the apses and prolonging the nave, making the church the largest ever built in Europe. Completion of Giotto's bell tower was put under the direction of Neri di Fioravanti and Taddeo Gaddi, and it was finished in eight years. Gaddi was Giotto's godson and, according to Giorgio Vasari, he was considered Giotto's most talented pupil.

During these years, it was Boccaccio who held aloft the guidon of Dante as the salvation for Florence. The *Decameron* was completed in 1353, a work wherein Boccaccio, in his own way, held the noses of Florentines to the odors of their deadly follies. In 1357 his *Life of Dante* was published. In 1359 he began an extended fight with the unresponsive Petrarch on the subject of the *Commedia*, a work that Petrarch disparaged. The year 1373 witnessed his daily lectures on the *Commedia*, and in that same year the government of Florence established a Chair for the promotion of the study of Dante at the University of Florence. Boccaccio was named its first occupant.

the lust for hereditary power on the part of the extended Angevin and Norman ruling families—all of these had combined to loot Europe and impoverish the populations in the decades leading up to 1348.

Many are familiar with the banking crash of 1345 that wiped out the Bardi, Peruzzi, and other banking houses. But that bursting of the *Trecento* financial bubble was itself the end-product of years of vicious economic thievery. For decades, caught in a web of usury and debt collection, Europe had been stripped of its agriculture and industry. The population was declining as early as the 1290s, food disappeared, famine and starvation spread throughout the continent, and whole cities and towns were depopulated: All of this prior to the arrival of the plague. By 1349 the devastation was complete.

One of the very first acts taken by the government of Florence, in 1351, as the population began to fight its way

Giotto's bell tower at the Basilica di Santa Maria del Fiore in Florence.

In 1367 occurred "one of the first events of the Italian Renaissance," as some have described it. A competition was held for architectural designs to move forward with the construction of the Florence Cathedral. The design that was accepted, a model by Neri di Fioravanti, was shocking and revolutionary. It abolished the original Gothic design of the Cathedral and eliminated all of the flying buttresses. Neri's model depicted a massive inner

Fresco by Domenico di Michelino in the Cathedral of Santa Maria del Fiore, showing Dante illuminating Florence with his Commedia.

dome, enclosed in a thinner outer shell, partly supported by the inner dome. Much as Dante had relegated Latin to the dead past, so Neri, in abandoning the Gothic style, announced the birth of a new era.

Neri's dome was to stand on an unbuttressed octagonal drum, and it would be the highest in the world. Neri's model was one of sweeping magnificence and beauty, but the most stunning aspect to it was that there was no known way to construct the dome he proposed. It simply could not be done; existing knowledge would not suffice. This was the great challenge, the Great Project, which was presented to the people of Florence, and it would take a *willful* breakthrough to a higher and more perfect understanding of the universe to overcome it. Thus the courage and the genius of Filippo Brunelleschi.[18]

In 1456, twenty years after the completion of Brunelleschi's dome, the workers of Santa Maria del Fiore—those who had built the dome—demanded that the finished Cathedral include the presence of Dante. Domenico di Michelino was commissioned for the work, and his fresco, *La Commedia Illumina Firenze* (The *Commedia* Illuminates Florence), is on the west wall of the Cathedral. The image of Dante towers over the scene, but in the background are Brunelleschi's dome, Giotto's *campanile,* the baptistery (where Dante was baptized), and the Bargello, the location of Giotto's 1337 fresco of Dante in Paradise.

Anyone who studies Michelino's fresco closely will see immediately that this is not an image of Florence "honoring" Dante. Rather, we see Dante, facing Flor-

---

18. Brunelleschi began work on the dome in 1420. He did not read

Latin; all of the designs and instructions for work on the dome were written in Dante's illustrious vernacular.

ence, displaying his *Commedia* and directing the attention of the City, through the motion of his right hand, to the display of Hell, Purgatory, and Paradise. It is not subtle. The *Commedia* is the pathway to Florence's salvation.

Out of the Blue

It is of course true that no creative personality stands alone. Shakespeare would not have been possible without Chaucer, nor Kepler without Cusa, nor Beethoven without Bach. Yet, true creativity is always something new, something which no one has ever conceived of or imagined before—new insights into the nature of the universe and mankind's role in that universe. In that regard, an idea intervenes that it would be a lawful action to abolish, once and for all, the use of the term "Renaissance." A literal English translation of the French word *renaissance* is "re-birth" or "revival," and the common understanding of the events of the 14th and 15th centuries is that European society was reborn through a rediscovery of the great literature and philosophy of the ancient Greek and Roman world.

The appellation "Renaissance" was first used by Jules Michelet in his 1856 *History of France*, and then became widely accepted after the publication of Jacob Burckhardt's *The Civilization of the Renaissance in Italy*, in 1860.

But look at the *Commedia*, look at Dante's *invention* of the Italian language "for the greater good." Nothing like this had existed before. No work in the ancient world, not even Homer's epics, compares with Dante's miracle of the *Commedia*. Look at Brunelleschi's dome, a work of true, creative science: Nothing like it exists amidst the marvels of ancient Greece, and Rome's Pantheon is crude and barbaric when compared to its magnificence. Brunelleschi and Dante unlocked previously hidden secrets and unleashed powers within the human species that were utterly new and revolutionary.

Dante insisted that Latin, the language of the educated class, and the language in which Augustine, Aquinas, and Cicero wrote, must be superseded by a language with greater power and potential. I believe it is no accident that in the *Commedia*, Virgil—at the apex of Latin literature—is not allowed to enter *Paradiso*, for Dante is posing an entirely new future to his audience.

I do not propose here a new substitute for the word "Renaissance," but it is clear that the acceptance of that term, and all of its implied meanings, obfuscates, perhaps deliberately, the nature of the new revolutionary discoveries which were accomplished during that era—

creative interventions that made possible new potentials for an increase in the productivity of the human species, an increase in man's realization of his true nature and his relation with the cosmos—potentials that had no prior existence.

It was not the "revival" of "ancient learning" which spurred the achievements of Dante, Giotto, and those who followed them; it was the urgent necessity to "create something new" if European society and culture were to survive the crisis of their time and to "break through" to a higher level of civilization. One might say that this creative power arises "out of thin air." Better to say that it dwells, usually dormant, within the recesses of each individual human soul.

None of this is said to denigrate what followed in the 15th Century, but not all of what followed was good. Many individuals, including Salutati, Nelli, Bracciolini, Bruni, and Chrysoloras were critical in the rediscovery and propagation of the works of Plato. Yet, the pernicious influence of classical Latin as the accepted medium for the elite remained, and the resurgence of oligarchical influence resulted in the follies of Ficino and particularly Pico della Mirandola. By the time of Nicholas of Cusa's great intervention and his own discoveries in science, the torchlight of Dante, Boccaccio, and Brunelleschi was already beginning to dim, so it would be left to Cusa to create anew, yet unknown breakthroughs for humanity.

It was the *Commedia* which created the means whereby Florence arose from the ashes. To read it today, even in a paltry English translation and out of time from its original intended audience, is still an experience of profound moral introspection and one of almost unbearable intellectual confrontation.

VI. The *Commedia*

To approach writing about Dante's *Commedia* fills this writer with dreadful trepidation. Obviously, a didactic approach will not do. It is also impossible to "answer all of the questions" or provide a definitive analysis. The best that may be done is to emulate Dante, and as he attempted to *approach* perfection in Paradiso, so we shall attempt to approach Dante here.

To aid in this effort, we shall employ a "ringer" and bring in the help of a friendly voice. In 1984 Lyndon LaRouche wrote "The Science of the Human Mind," within which there is a subsection, "Dante's

Dante addressing Pope Nicholas III in Malebolge, the eighth circle of Hell.

Commedia."[19] We quote here excerpts from what LaRouche wrote:

It is well-established, that the levels of development possible for the human individual fall among three general categories, as those three categories are described by the three successive canticles of Dante Alighieri's *Commedia*: "Inferno," "Purgatory," and "Paradise." The first is infantile man, the irrationalistic hedonist, whose philosophical world outloo k is that of David Hume, Adam Smith, Jeremy Bentham, and John Stuart Mill, among others. The second is of the philosophical world outlook best typified by Immanuel Kant, the Kant of his *Critique of Practical Reason*. To identify the third, preliminary discussion is required.

The fact of our individual mortality ought

19. 'Dante's Commedia,' in "The Science of the Human Mind," by Lyndon LaRouche, *The Campaigner*, Special Supplement, February 1984.

to impress each of us, at some point in our pre-adolescent or adolescent development, that those hedonistic pleasures whose memory exists chiefly in the experience of our own flesh, die in our grave with us. To live a life serving the pursuit of such individual pleasure is to die as a beast dies, leaving nothing after us better in principle than what is bequeathed to us by the beast who died yesterday in the slaughter-house. The survivors consume the remains, and after that, there is nothing of importance in the matter of society. The beginning of wisdom is to reflect upon this lesson, that we not waste our brief lives living and dying like mere beasts.

To accomplish this, we must find a means to make our having once lived of durable advantage to both our contemporaries and our society's posterity in general. We must make some contribution to the advancement of the human condition. We must develop our potentialities accordingly. This broad, preliminary answer poses a second question, a deeper question: How can we have foreknowledge of what will be of such advantage to mankind? . . .

The case of the individual in "Purgatory" helps to instruct us, that to realize the higher self-interest in the Good, it is not sufficient to be able to recognize the Good descriptively, or even to be inspired by the desire to achieve what he describes as Good. We must become Good; we must be governed in impulses respecting our immediately personal self-interest by that Good. That Good must become our immediate self-interest, our immediate motivation in every aspect of personal life.

To achieve that congruence of personal, self-interested impulses and service of the Good, is the condition of "Paradise." . . .

Reason itself cannot define sanity. Without the motive to submit one's will to Reason, the individual's will will be submitted more or less fully to the bestial ordering of impulses of wretches of the "Inferno"—or, perhaps, of "Purgatory." Without a love for Reason more powerful than the infantile hedonism to which one is born, Reason will not be attained.

In that sense, Reason and the love of Reason, and corresponding hostility toward existentialist irrationalism, are the essential characteristics of the sane adult mind. Any deviation from that standard, that "norm" if one insists, is psychopathology. The science of the human mind is a study of the methods by which that indicated psycho-pathology is overcome. ...

This ennobled state of the majority of citizens is characterized, relative to "Purgatory," by a shift of the sense of personal identity, and personal self-interest within society; to the individual's true self-interest as a world-historical personality, a personality whose immediate motive of self-interest is the development and exercise of the powers to contribute a durable Good to his or her society over succeeding generations to come. It is that shift of the cathexis of sense of personal identity and self-interest within the personality, which defines "Paradise."

The Light of Reason

With those words by LaRouche to guide us—but before we turn to the heart of the matter—a few things should be said about the language and imagery of the *Commedia*.

The language of the *Commedia* is extraordinary. Dante abandons completely his earlier use of the sonnet form as well as that of the beautiful *canzoni* of the *Convivio*. He is not writing lyric poetry here. For the *Commedia*, Dante invents "out of the blue" an entire, new poetic language. He creates the *terza rima* rhyme scheme of aba-bcb-cdc ..., thus the last word of the second line within each tercet becomes the basis for rhyming the first and third lines of the next tercet. Each line has eleven syllables (thus it is called hendecasyllabic), but there is no set meter (such as iambic pentameter). The rhythm, the inner dynamic, and the force of Dante's language in the *Commedia* is strikingly different from his earlier poetry.

Throughout the one hundred cantos, the *terza rima* propels the reader forward. It is relentless. The absence of meter allows a freedom in expression, as action or contemplation is slowed or speeded up, or the mood is shifted—but never allowed to rest. One might say that

---

Shelley on Dante

Dante understood the secret things of love even more than Petrarch. His *Vita Nuova* is an inexhaustible fountain of purity of sentiment and language: it is the idealized history of that period, and those intervals of his life which were dedicated to love. His apotheosis of Beatrice in Paradise, and the gradations of his own love and her loveliness—by which as by steps he feigns himself to have ascended to the throne of the Supreme Cause—is the most glorious imagination of modern poetry. The acutest critics have justly reversed the judgement of the vulgar, and the order of the great acts of the 'Divine Drama,' in the measure of the admiration which they accord to Hell, Purgatory, and Paradise. The latter is a perpetual hymn of everlasting love. Love, which found a worthy poet in Plato alone of all the ancients, has been celebrated by a chorus of the greatest writers of the renovated world; and the music has penetrated the caverns of society, and its echoes still drown the dissonance of arms and superstition.

Dante was the first awakener of entranced Europe; he created a language, in itself music and persuasion, out of a chaos of inharmonious barbarisms. He was the congregator of those great spirits who presided over the resurrection of learning; the Lucifer of that starry flock which in the Thirteenth Century shone forth from republican Italy, as from a heaven, into the darkness of the benighted world. His very words are instinct with spirit; each is as a spark, a burning atom of inextinguishable thought; and many yet lie covered in the ashes of their birth, and pregnant with a lightning which has yet found no conductor. All high poetry is infinite; it is as the first acorn, which contained all oaks potentially. Veil after veil may be undrawn, and the inmost naked beauty of the meaning never exposed. A great poem is a fountain for ever overflowing with the waters of wisdom and delight; and after one person and one age has exhausted all its divine effluence which their peculiar relations enable them to share, another and yet another succeeds, and new relations are ever developed, the source of an unforeseen and an unconceived delight.

A Defence of Poetry
—Percy Bysshe Shelley, 1821

Dante uses all of the vocal registers, low to high, and all of the moods, from the ridiculous to the sublime. At times the language is almost violent, at other times it is excruciatingly tragic, or contemplative, and as Dante begins to ascend through the increasingly brilliant vision of Paradise, his language takes on a beauty that is unequaled.

Light is one of Dante's paramount metaphors in the *Commedia*: *luce* (light), *raggio* (radiance), *splendore* (splendor). Hell is governed by darkness, which deepens as Dante descends. It is dismal, barren, hideous. This is not the "fiery pit" of legend; Lucifer's lair is black, icy, evil. In Purgatory the darkness begins to lift as Dante moves through shadows. As he ascends the mountain, the shadows clear in the light of the Sun. Gradually, the domination of the senses which characterized Hell—where Dante weeps, faints, and must be steadied by Virgil—fades away. He is freeing his will from bestial senses, which culminates in the clarity of the earthly paradise.

This is not simply sunlight. It is not sensual, visual light. It is heavenly light, the *prime mover*, which is propelling him upward.

The realms of light begin to change as Dante moves upward through Paradise, and with each change, his inner and outer vision, his intellect, his power of reason, grow, as he absorbs the true nature of the universe. He travels to a state "beyond metaphor, but one to which all metaphor aspires." In the *Paradiso*, Dante's mind is fully purified and enlarged to conceive of the inner truth of creation—"moving from one mind to a 'higher' mind." His will, once feeble at the beginning of his journey, is now in unity with his intellect, and both are enveloped within an all-encompassing love. Our ability to create depends on our willingness (our *will,* driven by love) to enter the Kingdom of Heaven: the separation of the will from the senses and the joining of the will to the divine creative process.

Dante's Journey

The *Commedia* is set in the year 1300, when Dante was 34 years old. As anyone with even scant knowledge of the *Commedia* knows, it begins with Dante at a moment of great crisis, a moment—as Dante says—when "the straight way was lost." He knows not how he got there: He is confused and distressed, and his heart is "pierced with fear."

It is at this moment that Virgil arrives, sent by Beatrice, to lead him on a journey. It begins with the entry into Hell—*Lasciate ogne speranza, voi ch'intrate* ("Abandon all hope, ye who enter here"), and Dante's senses are immediately assaulted by anguished screams.

Dante and Virgil see Bertran de Born, holding his severed head, in Malebolge.

This first arena is the place for the Uncommitted, those who, in life, took no sides.[20]

From there, Dante and Virgil descend through the nine circles of Hell. Suffice it to say that this is the realm of bestial sense-perception—of the senses. It is the fitting home—as LaRouche emphasizes—of Adam Smith, whose theory of economics, now hegemonic in the trans-Atlantic world—is based on the animalistic "pursuit of pleasure and the avoidance of pain." It is the home for all those who have closed themselves off from their *agapic* inner potential.

For the entirety of his sojourn through Hell, Dante himself is frequently overcome—anguished. He is profoundly affected by what he sees and experiences. This is not compassion; it is a product of the anchor of sense-

---

20. Franklin Roosevelt referenced this punishment in his speech to the 1936 Democratic Convention, when he said, "Governments can err, presidents do make mistakes, but the immortal Dante tells us that Divine justice weighs the sins of the cold-blooded and the sins of the warm-hearted on different scales. Better the occasional faults of a government that lives in a spirit of charity than the consistent omissions of a government frozen in the ice of its own indifference." Both Robert and John Kennedy also frequently cited this lesson on moral indifference, and Martin Luther King featured it in his 1967 sermon at the Ebenezer Baptist Church, "Why I Am Opposed to the War in Vietnam."

perception which still occupies Dante's soul.

As they descend, Dante and Virgil pass through the circles of Lust, Gluttony, Greed, and Wrath, all in Upper Hell. In Canto IX they enter the *City of Dis* which contains Lower Hell, inhabited by the Heretics and the Violent. As they descend, the punishments become worse, because the inhabitants are further and further away from God. In Canto XVIII they enter *Malebolge*, the Eighth Circle, given over to those guilty of Fraud. This circle is subdivided into ten rings (*Bolgia*), and here the punishments inflicted are terrifying.[21]

Corrupt politicians are immersed in a lake of boiling pitch, guarded by demons called the Malebranche who tear them to pieces with their claws if they catch them above the surface of the pitch. The Falsifiers are afflicted with horrible diseases and lie screaming in stench, thirst, filth, and darkness. Some lie prostrate while others run through the pit, tearing others to pieces. The Sowers of Discord are hacked and mutilated for all eternity by a large demon wielding a bloody sword.

The final descent is to the Ninth Circle, the icy lake of *Cocytus*, where the Treacherous are punished. In the very center of Hell, condemned for committing the ultimate sin—personal treachery against God—is Lucifer. Lucifer is not the "ruler" of Hell; he is a giant, terrifying beast trapped waist-deep in the ice, fixed and suffering. His punishment is most extreme because he is the worst sinner.

Redemption

Now I shall sing the second kingdom,
there where the soul of man is cleansed,
made worthy to ascend to Heaven.

At about 6:00 p.m. on Saturday evening, Virgil and Dante make their escape from Hell, passing through the center of the universe and of gravity, and emerging into the Southern Hemisphere at dawn of Easter Sunday. They are now at Mount Purgatory.

In *Purgatorio* Dante begins a process of ascending from the corporeal to the spiritual. This is not a discussion of an "afterlife"; it is one of atonement, moving from a state of misery to bliss. One of the characteristics of this new dimension is Dante's frequent discussion of astronomy, the visible stars, and the position of the Sun.[22]

Dante and Beatrice (left), in "Paradiso," Canto III.

Dante's eyes are being drawn upward.[23]

This is the arena of atonement, purification, redemption, but one where the self is still being drawn in two directions, and where the union of the will with the Good is imperfect.

As Lyndon LaRouche stated in the work cited above, "The case of the individual in 'Purgatory,' helps to instruct us, that to realize the higher self-interest in the Good, it is not sufficient to be able to recognize the Good descriptively, or even to be inspired by the desire to achieve what he describes as Good. We must become Good."

In Purgatory Dante hears the canzone, *Amor che ne la mente mi ragiona*, as well as the hymns *Salve Regina*

---

21. Dante places three Popes in Malebolge, and five Popes in all are in the *Inferno*, together with many of Dante's enemies, all of whom are representative of the evil oligarchical paradigm that Dante battled.

22. There are many references and discussions in the *Commedia* on astronomy, optics, language, geography, and other aspects of science. In

his in-depth description of Italian geography, as well as in his depiction of characters from every region—having them speak in their own dialects—he is, in fact, "creating" Italy. Dante also gives the circumference of the Earth as 20,400 miles (the actual circumference is 24,901 miles), which has led some scholars to posit that this was based on his study of the works of Ahmad ibn Muhammad ibn Kathir al-Farghani, the Arab astronomer of the Ninth Century.

23. The ability of Dante's message to survive in even the unlikeliest of places is remarkable. It is almost unknown today that the first European feature-length film every produced, and the first international film "blockbuster," was a silent adaptation of Dante's *Inferno*. Titled *L'Inferno*, it was released in 1911, four years prior to D.W. Griffith's *Birth of a Nation*. All of the intertitles used in the film are verbatim selections of cantos from Dante's *Inferno* in the original Florentine vernacular (in the United States, the intertitles were from the Cary translation). The sets and scenery were created using the illustrations of Gustave Doré. The film grossed more than $2 million in the United States alone.

and *Te Lucis ante Terminum,* and there is much of beauty in the surroundings. Nevertheless, Purgatory is a place of struggle: The angel who stands guard at Peter's Gate uses two keys, silver (remorse) and gold (reconciliation), to open the gate, and both are necessary for redemption.

In Purgatory are to be found those guilty of Late-Repentance, Pride, Envy, Wrath, Sloth, Avarice, Gluttony, and Lust. Many of these are transgressions which are also condemned in Hell, but the difference here is one of intention. Those in Purgatory committed their sins through differing aspects of perverted, imperfect love. The punishments of Purgatory—though not of the nature of the Inferno—are severe: the Envious wear penitential grey cloaks, and their eyes are sewn shut with iron wire; the Wrathful walk in acrid smoke; the Gluttonous are starved in the presence of trees whose fruit is forever out of reach.

All of those in Purgatory may leave voluntarily— willfully—but only when they have corrected the flaw within themselves, when they have moved beyond the lure and trap of sense perception. Thus, the process of self-perfection is willful.

Traveling through Purgatory, Dante and Virgil are constantly moving upward, and with that ascent, the air clears, the light is brighter, and Dante's intellect is less clouded. Shortly before sunset, they reach the final terrace, just below the Earthly Paradise. As the Sun sets, they lie down to sleep.

In the Earthly Paradise, in a very dramatic scene, Dante is reunited with Beatrice, and then he is drawn through two rivers—the River Lethe, which erases the memory of past sin, and the River Eunoë, from which he drinks, restoring his memories of goodness and preparing him for the ascent to Heaven. This is no longer the Beatrice of the *Vita Nuova.* Neither the romantic nor sensual love of Dante's adolescence is present. Neither is this the abstract Lady Philosophy of the *Convivio.* In one sense, we might say that Beatrice has been redeemed, and her person has risen to a state of Divine Goodness.

Paradise[24]

The glory of Him who moves all things
pervades the universe and shines

---

24. All quotations from the *Paradiso* are taken from the English translation done by Robert and Jean Hollander, and are freely available on the website of the Princeton Dante Project. Dante's original Italian is also available on the Princeton site.

in one part more and in another less.

I was in that heaven which receives
more of His light. He who comes down from there
can neither know nor tell what he has seen,

for, drawing near to its desire,
so deeply is our intellect immersed
that memory cannot follow after it.

Nevertheless, as much of the holy kingdom
as I could store as treasure in my mind
shall now become the subject of my song.

Beatrice leads Dante through the Ring of Fire, which separates Purgatory from Paradise. Paradise is depicted as a series of concentric spheres surrounding the Earth, defined by the Moon, Mercury, Venus, the Sun, Mars, Jupiter, Saturn, the Fixed Stars, the *Primum Mobile,* and finally, the *Empyrean.*

Dante's intention, his language and imagery throughout *Paradiso,* is so magnificent and so dense, that, at this point, I find it impossible to convey, in prose, Dante's idea. At the risk of "ruining the ending" for those who have not yet read the *Commedia,* the remainder of this section will consist largely of Dante's own words, or rather, an English translation of them.

Note that in the very first sphere, the author Dante devotes one and one-half cantos to a dialogue between himself and Beatrice on the subject of the Freedom of the Will. This is an extensive discussion, and Dante takes a series of words, including *volontà, voglia, voler, invoglia,* and *volontade,* and examines their shades of meaning. The subject is the will's direction of human love to divine ends, and that this is the natural condition of Paradise. Dante says:

"The greatest gift that God in His largesse
gave to creation, the most attuned
to His goodness and that He accounts most dear,

"was the freedom of the will:
all creatures possessed of intellect,
all of them and they alone, were and are so endowed."

The entirety of *Paradiso* is an examination of self-perfection. Ever-ascending, ever-rising, being drawn closer and closer to the Prime Mover of all things universal. Dante and Beatrice move through the circles of the Wise, the Warriors of the Faith, and the Just Rulers. Although Dante does not state this explicitly, it is very clear that almost all of the individuals they encounter had, themselves, to pass through Purgatory and willfully embrace a process of self-perfection, and Dante presents this as a challenge to the reader. In Canto X he says:

Stay on your bench now, reader,
thinking of the joy you have but tasted,
if, well before you tire, you would be happy.

I have set your table. From here on feed yourself,
for my attention now resides
in that matter of which I have become the scribe.

It is Beatrice who leads from good
to better so suddenly that her action
has no measurement in time.

Whatever I saw within the sun, how shining
it must have been, for, when I entered,
it revealed itself, not by color, but by light.

Were I to call on genius, skill, and practice,
I could not ever tell how this might be imagined.
Enough if one believes and longs to see it.

And if the powers of our imagination
are too earthbound for such height, it is no wonder,
for eye has never seen light brighter than the sun.

And in Canto XIV, Dante makes it very clear whence the motive for such willful improvement derives:

"Just as long as the festival of Paradise
shall last, that is how long our love
shall dress us in this radiance.

"Its brightness answers to our ardor,
the ardor to our vision, and that is given
in greater measure of grace than we deserve.

"so that the light, granted to us freely
by the Highest Good, shall increase,
the light that makes us fit to see Him.

"From that light, vision must increase,
and love increase what vision kindles,
and radiance increase, which comes from love."

In Canto XXII they enter the Fixed Stars, where Dante is tested on Faith, Hope, and Love by Saints Peter, James, and John, and through the mouth of Peter, Dante delivers his most withering attack on the corruption, simony, and bribery rampant within the upper echelons of the Church.

From the Fixed Stars, Beatrice and Dante next enter the *Primum Mobile* (the "first moved"). As they enter, Beatrice says:

Dante and Beatrice in the Primum Mobile.

"The nature of the universe, which holds
the center still and moves all else around it,
starts here as from its boundary line.

"This heaven has no other where
but in the mind of God, in which is kindled
the love that turns it and the power it pours down.

"Light and love enclose it in a circle,
as it contains the others. Of that girding
He that girds it is the sole Intelligence.

"Its motion is not measured by another's,
but from it all the rest receive their measures,
even as does ten from its half and from its fifth.

"How time should have its roots in a single flower pot
and its foliage in all the others
may now become quite clear to you."

And then, as they are departing from the *Primum Mobile*, Beatrice says,

With the voice and bearing of a guide
who has discharged his duty, she began: "We have
* issued*
from the largest body to the Heaven of pure light,

"light intellectual, full of love,
love of true good, full of joy,
joy that surpasses every sweetness.

"Here you shall see both soldieries of Paradise,
one of them in just such form
as you shall see it at the final judgment."

Like sudden lightning that confounds
the faculty of sight, depriving eyes
of taking in the clearest objects,

thus did a living light shine all around me,
leaving me so swathed in the veil of its effulgence
that I saw nothing else.

Finally, in the *Empyrean*, Dante is able to gaze directly upon God. Dante's writing, and his description of what he sees, is so overwhelming and so beautiful that I must restrain an almost overpowering desire to print it here, but that would be unforgivable. Every human being must read this for himself or herself. Every person must be given the opportunity to traverse the path that Dante walked, and each individual must make his or her own way to the *Empyrean*.

VII. The Dawn of an Era

We live today in a trans-Atlantic culture that is filled with rage. The problem we face is not simply one of hedonism or pessimistic existentialism. Among the women, the men, and individuals of every generation there is deep rage at what has been denied them, what has been lost, the humanity which has been erased. People everywhere are yearning for something better. This is why the lesson of Dante is so critical—to give back to people the hope they have lost, the sense of what it means to be truly human.

We are at the cusp of two divergent paths. One direction leads to a future of war, chaos, and economic collapse. The second is best exemplified by the brilliant initiatives emanating from the Belt and Road idea. The partnership that is developing among a growing number of nations for economic development—and for a New Paradigm—is now the hope for all humanity. Within this framework, as stated at the beginning of this article, many have encouraged a "dialogue of civilizations" to further the process of worldwide peace and economic development. This is where the writings and the mind of Dante are so indispensable.

There are two aspects to this. The first is that a dialogue of civilizations must be based on what is best in those civilizations. This, in turn, requires that people in Asia, Africa, and elsewhere—as well as within the trans-Atlantic community itself—must learn what the true Western Culture is. It is not what most people think. They have been lied to! It has been hidden from them.

In 1763 the British Empire emerged as the dominant force on this planet, and it has ruled the world ever since, joined after 1945 by its now-corrupted American partners. As the saying goes, "It is the victors who write the history books," and over the last two and a half centuries it has been the representatives of that empire who have not only written the political histories, but who have imposed the values, culture, and so-called science of their own imperial worldview.

Adam Smith, David Hume, Jeremy Bentham, and John Stuart Mill all express that degenerate worldview, and all will eternally inhabit Dante's *Inferno*. The same is true for Bertrand Russell, John Dewey, John Von Neumann, and filth such as Nietzsche and Richard Wagner. These have nothing to do with Western Culture, except as an oozing, puss-encrusted corrupt disease upon it. They are representatives of the anti-human world outlook of Empire. They are enemies of the upward progress of humanity.

The wonders that flowed from Florence, the creation of the American Republic, and the creativity of Beethoven all flow from the view of the nature of man as recognized by Dante. Cusa, Kepler, Leibniz, Einstein, Hamilton, Lincoln, Schiller, Shakespeare, Mozart, Schubert, and Shelley—these and others exist in what Lyndon LaRouche has called the *Simultaneity of Eternity*. The sanctity of man's identity and the willful upward perfectability of mankind's role in the universe: This is the true Western cultural tradition, and no one should ever be allowed to misrepresent or hijack it.

In one very specific sense, at the highest level, there are no distinct, "separate" civilizations, and this is where Dante enters in again. What Dante puts forth, in the *Commedia*, is the universal nature of every human being ever born, anywhere in the world. No truly great civilization has ever arisen, no profound culture has ever been promulgated, which did not have, at its heart, the view of humanity and human potential expressed by Dante. Ultimately, we are not so different after all.

Dante fought for human redemption. He saw the "light behind the light." So should we all.

AN AUTOBIOGRAPHICAL MEMORANDUM

My Science & Our Society

Lyndon H. LaRouche, Jr.

During this past week, I took the occasion to present a long-standing, personal conviction respecting the meaning of science. I argued, as I presented the case to some relevant associates, that the time has come to throw archaic truisms respecting science to the proverbial winds.

I avowed, that there exists only one foundation for the foundations of mankind's knowledge of science: the self-development of the human species itself: the meaning of the human mind itself, a meaning which is bounded by the progress of mankind's conquest of successively more and more of the unknowns of mankind's coming into evidence of the organization of what we know as our immediate universe. The rest were merely fictions rooted in silly fantasies.

The notion of merely abstract theories of the universe, has been implicitly a disaster, a wickedly awful waste of human time and energies. Happily, in the living history of scientific knowledge, there exists a kernel of uncertainties which, by means of a process of experimental discoveries, unveils more and more of the universal mystery which envelopes a process of human knowledge respecting the universe which we inhabit.

Actually, knowledge to that effect was already very ancient, and includes the most rudimentary distinctions of the human species from all known others, this far. On this account, modern science, notably since the work of Filippo Brunelleschi, Cardinal Nicholas of Cusa, and their followers, the foundations of a modern science was supplied, by them, and, chiefly, thereafter, to those who followed the trail which they had (so-to-speak) "blazed through" the fields and forests of a new, Classical scientific method encompassing the topical themes of Classical artistic and physical-scientific domains, that crafted as a unitary conception.

Human knowledge defines itself, not through sense-perception as such; but, through the conquest of experimental knowledge, beginning the solid principle of mankind's most crucial discovery, that our species has not been that of an animal (excepting the perverted opinions of idiots, or their like).

From a modern scientific standpoint in evidence, these are matters which actually mark the distinction of the human species from all presently known, other living creatures.

For example:

In retrospect, this standpoint of our view of the uniqueness of mankind among presently known forms of life, can be located in the essential distinction of mind from the mere brain on which the biological support for human mental processes, perhaps unfortunately, uniquely depends. The conclusion is, that, that distinction is of fundamental importance and scientific significance, alike, a significance which can not be attributed to merely sense-perception as such; but, is, rather, nearer to man's best-grounded knowledge, that away from the principled distinctions of the mere beasts, or the merely misguided approximations of what many consider, erroneously, as acceptable religious belief: in short, the human mind.

The crucial distinction of the human mind, is, in other words, that we must regard confidence in sense-perception as such, with a certain profoundly-rooted distaste. This echoes the famous German motion-picture scheme of 1960: "Die Hauptsache ist der Effekt!"[1] We know effects, not simple certainties; these effects

---

1. A 1960 German satirical comedy film.

Creative Commons

Filippo Brunelleschi (1377-1446) (statue shown), in his design of the dome of the Cathedral of Florence, "crushed mere mathematics with pioneering in a truly physical science based on principles of systemic insight, as with the exemplary case of his revolutionary design of for the principles of modern physics, rather than merely experiments as such."

Pennie Sabel

acquire knowledge of those universal effects (i.e., principles), not as interpretations of sense-perceptions *per se.* Such were the necessary methods of the true founders of modern science, the Golden Renaissance geniuses, Filippo Brunelleschi, Cardinal Nicholas of Cusa, and Cusa's most notable scientific heir, Johannes Kepler.

Some Broad Considerations

It must now be recognized, that sense-perception is merely sense-perception: a shadow cast without an inherently known substance-in-fact. Hence, in any actually competent expression of modern science, true knowledge, is not to be based on mere hands-on experiment, as such; but, rather, it is but the seemingly mysterious power of provable universal physical principles of experimental knowledge, as such: never statistical deductions.

This notion of principle stands in opposition to mere experiment as such, as all of the greatest among modern scientists had an understanding of what is the notion of an actual principle as such. Johannes Kepler's greatest achievement was of that nature, in his discovery of a lawful principle of Solar space-time, an outstanding example of the meaning of principle in science.

That principle, as Kepler himself had emphasized, had been located in the work of Nicholas of Cusa. The same was true, of Cusa's relatively biological senior in physical-science designs: Filippo Brunelleschi, with Brunelleschi's methods for the founding of modern physical science: a science which echoed the unique methods of Eratosthenes, as Eratosthenes typifies that in his measuring of the Earth, and related achievements.

Brunelleschi went further, and deeper into the mysteries, crushing mere mathematics with pioneering in a truly physical science based on principles of systemic insight, as with the exemplary case of his revolutionary design for the principles of modern physics, rather than merely experiments as such: as shown with the science expressed by such as the great Cathedral of

provide the basis in experimental proofs for a useful approximation of man's actually relative degree of certainties. True principles, defined in actually scientific terms of reference, are invariables, not solutions for mere equations. They may be expressed in terms of approximation, but, they remain principles in the same sense that Max Planck and Albert Einstein defined physical principles for the really intelligent people during the time leading into the best Twentieth-Century standards for actually thermonuclear physical-scientific practice.

Actually, sense perceptions are effects, not self-evident truths in and of themselves. The meaning of those effects must be adduced from the powers of mankind to

Florence and the miraculous power of the Pazzi chapel (both of which cases fascinated me scientifically, in my own time, in my collaboration with certain leading Italian scientists working in deeper investigations into the nature of these as deep, scientific discoveries of principle from the Golden Renaissance).

The Evil of Euclid:

The fraud which I had recognized in my first encounter with Euclidean geometry, in my experience with secondary education, had contributed greatly to my consequently permanent contempt for "practical" opinion. Contempt for Euclid helped me greatly, not only for reason of his awful scientific fraud; but, by warning me to learn the signal lessons of Eratosthenes, as representing a revolutionary method of truth for all physical science.

Francesco Caprioli

A family tradition: Lyndon LaRouche's father and grandfather worked in the shoe industry, but his own inclinations, he writes, were "very different." Here, Lyndon and Helga LaRouche visit an engineering school in Ascoli Piceno, Italy, in 2002, where LaRouche is discussing a new production technology with staff members.

The complementary, leading influence on my direction of investigations, followed the method of Plato's fairly well; but, my original study of Plato was more limited, this because I had already grasped, in the course of my secondary and later education, the implication of the fraud of Euclidean geometry, which had put me on the track for seeing the importance of Plato's own work. The case of my "seemingly impulsive" recognition of Euclid's fraud, had put the proverbial "fire in my belly;" I was already convinced, as if in advance, that Plato represented "my side" of the cause. I was, in fact, already a persuaded Promethean, in effect, throughout the course of my education since during the time of my secondary education, i.e., which is to say, the process of entry into puberty.

For those reasons, I was always enraged, thereafter, by the formalities of a customarily taught geometry in both my secondary school, and university experiences. The evidence of Euclid's fraud, in my adolescent consideration of high-rise steel construction, had impelled me to seek out, and, to defy sources which implicitly echoed the systemic, known hoax inherent in the Euclidean method. This, has stood me in good stead ever since.

Thus, I had avoided the popularized academic follies in which many of my contemporaries had fallen, entrapped by their own worship of "false gods." With Gottfried Leibniz, for example, I was at home; and, later, with much of Gauss, and Riemann: which for me, was that the latter were a pair of close collaborators respecting the principles of physical science broadly considered, and, thence, since Planck and Einstein, in the qualitatively principled features of their general, revolutionary contributions during the 1890s and beyond.

How My Career Had Begun:

I have had certain distinguishing examples of such principles as these, in my own circumstances as a child, youth, and, then, my adulthood, later.

My paternal grandfather and father had been, among their other skills, rooted in the particular professionalism of the shoe manufacturing process, and with some related expertise in the technologies of that industry. They were both qualified experts in the underlying features of that manufacturing skill. But, my father and I were very different in our inclinations, otherwise.

We had some occasionally excellent cooperation, but, relatively, preferably at a comfortable distance, psychologically, from childhood, to the end of our association. This was, in effect of practice, largely because he persistently sought to push me to submit to choices where I had no desire to go.[2]

My own inclination was always at a distance from the hurly-burly of simply hands-on practice, a difference which was premised, for me, for the sake of deeper considerations: even where our activities, as parent and son, might seem to converge otherwise. He preferred practice for its own sake, and the prospect of its gains; I preferred scientific practice in pursuit of general principles of science, in matters of underlying principle. What that interested for me was a hatred of cook-book science-education of the typically available secondary school and university. My revulsion was not one of desire, but a sense that "I should not be here;" I did not believe in "them." I hated the folly of popular belief in the cultic academic certainties based on the principle of regurgitating what one had been taught; I wished a truth which were rightly known to me, as my own: not hand-me-down intellectual costumes.

So, by a complex of circumstances, I was, in due course, as a young adult professional, co-opted, partly as a matter of recovering from a rather prolonged, serious hepatitis attack, into the modest role of assisting in a management assignment, to help out a friend with largely inherited business problems. I took to the profession which that implied, like a proverbial duck who had been waiting for the discovery of water. This occupation projected me, soon, into my later role of a management consultant for a large such organization (of which I did not always approve), and soon gained a promotion to a part of the executive occupied with methods of scientific forecasting specialties, as I was at some times a key figure of that firm's staff.

Up to a certain point, I had been more than merely highly successful as a professional, and, then a member of the executive staff. My achievements were most actively accelerated during a period in which I served as

the de facto available scientist and general "brain-truster." My career had progressed rapidly, until I came into a not-really-chance meeting with the FBI (within the New York City Chanin Building's bank of elevator shafts), an FBI which wished to engage me, outside my more regular duties, in a project which I brushed off, by telling the agent, that his organization's proposed project was a worthless waste of our mutual time; but that I would gladly entertain assisting in anything worth considering as a more serious investigation. That was, in short, the end of my then-accustomed career for a period of duration of several, or more years—that is to say, in my role as an executive of the consulting firm which had then, actually, employed me prior to my run-ins with the FBI. (I subsisted as a part-time consultant.)

However, by that time, I had already produced the best economic forecasting performance in the industry, by pin-pointing the exact dates when a major industrial crisis of that decade would break out. I was out of the consulting firm (courtesy of the FBI); but, nevertheless, still one of the best economic forecasters, as I had been, already, in 1957, then and later, in the field. Soon, during the early 1970s, I was given the opportunity to prove my point. Soon, by Summer 1971, I had soon proven myself, thoroughly, as the best economic forecaster in both the United States (and also) Britain, too. (Not as much to my own credit, but, rather, the incredibility of my professional rivals. Life, I have found, is often like that.)

The significance of that choice of profession, as an economic forecaster, is that it is, implicitly the top of the list in terms of the career functions. Very few professionals are really competent in dealing with subjects of that nature, or on that scale, as I was to prove that fact in the Summer and Autumn of 1971 and, repeatedly, beyond. Mere statisticians are flops in that category of professional functions. I have been (scientifically) the best in that field since, certainly, since, in fact, about 1968-1971, and, soon, that pretty much, implicitly, internationally: that for the English-speaking world, at first, but, also in some other sectors of the planet, not long thereafter. My merely apparent disadvantage, has been, that the biggest success of a professional in my ranks, could, and did lead to those foreseen disasters later experienced by me, which had been caused by those who wished me to be suddenly highly unwanted, not only in my professional field, but in my very existence, as well. This is, nonetheless, still my profession,

---

2. Among other things, he refused to consider the fact that I was destined to be a bass-baritone stentor, not a tenor, like him. As genetically proud as he was, he could never forgive me for that reason, alone, and made his point very clear. (My maternal grandfather, a small, but potent Scotsman by birth, was, also, unquestionably, nothing other than a bass.) Since my surgery, more than a decade ago, my singing-voice was gone forever, when combined with the effects of pipe-smoking. (Nothing would prevent me from having, incurably "bass motives" within my soul.) My paternal great-grandfather and grandfather, were from Rimouski, in Canada; my grandfather was a musician (like his father, a maker of violins), and their careers as specialists in shoe manufacturing, The French and Scottish roots of my paternal ancestries had overlapped something in the vicinity of southern coastal Massachusetts.

and I am still one of the best at it, as to be known still today, as events have demonstrated repeatedly.

On the Subject of My Profession:

The crucial importance of that aspect of my personal history, defines that which I do: as earlier, and as now. It is a function suited best to the highest rank of insight into the principles of economy, from a top-down view of prospects over time, and, that. over a nation, or a set of nations. It is necessary to see almost everything from the veritable top-down, locally, not as if from below. In other words: the practical significance for persons in such positions as my own particular profession, is that we see things from the top down (sometimes) for better, and, more frequently, for worse—the latter as Wall Street types do. The latter, tend to see the world from a relatively top-down standpoint of reference, as I do, still now, but, as if by habit. In fact, I am better, and they are terribly wrong; the difference is, that they are inherently wrong in their habituated methods of judgment (I have always trusted Alexander Hamilton on this account).

My particular speciality is a forecasting which approaches, all of my professional achievements as a economist, as, also my achievements and effectively global-strategic, top-down, outlook. I have been very good at that, considering the limitations which, presently, age, and related circumstances place upon the time and energy available to me as resources in practice. Today, it is like being a ninety-year-plus, great-grandfather type on the implied board of directors: hopefully, not-too-grouchy, but, also, not to continue my practice for much longer.

In my age, profession, and condition; the rule must be, get it done, but don't wait too long to do it, if you wish yourself to get the job actually done!

I could say a lot about that; but, having said as much as I have spoken here, this far, that is enough to set the stage for describing my role I play within the working bounds of this present report.

My responsibilities at this moment are momentous; if my present exertions were successful, and were I able to continue to function under the present intensity of my duties, I would, otherwise, "naturally" tend to a less intensive role in time and exertions alike. I am still vigorously capable for dealing with tough intellectual situations within the compass of my present knowledge and related habits, and in matters of relevant scientific discoveries in which I play a part; but, my present situation is necessarily temporary in terms of times what is to be counted down: that, biologically, on this scale, medical developments considered: plus, or minus.

The point of this report, is that there are certain principled issues of scientific method, in respect to which, I touch matters at a relatively very high level of intellectual and related competence for these times. My function, here, in this report, is to present several points of reference which have a sweeping implication for the relatively immediate present and future needs of nations, including my own. Part of this, is simply a continuation of that which I have come to do, which is essentially my own department; however, there are certain, few matters, in which my principled achievements are, both, still advancing, and more or less unique under the present conditions of presently catastrophic global crisis. I am on record, repeatedly, as (in fact) among the best economic (and related forecasters) alive, still today; that is my profession; that is who I am. The present threat of human thermonuclear extinction, is a highly relevant example of how I respond to crisis; I find myself, repeatedly, being a strategist. That is also in the nature of the subject of this present report, as now follows.

I. What Is Science Actually?

The teaching of the practice of mathematics, that usually done on the silly presumption that it is a foundation of scientific practice, is among the commonplace signs of rampant folly among both the so-called "scientific," and the lower professions of both financial accounting, as in the inherently crooked Wall Street practice known as "usury." The true facts of the subject-matter, were settled, for all competent minds today, by the standards set, implicitly, in Treasury Secretary Alexander Hamilton's four principles of the physical economy of that American System of society which had been established within an environment created under the leadership of Benjamin Franklin.[3] That means the profound American cultural victory over that of the British empire of that time; and, the genius exemplified by the unique discoveries made by the first Ad-

---

3. See (1) Report on Public Credit (1790); (2) Report on a National Bank (1790); (3) Opinion on the Constitutionality of a National Bank (1791); (4) Report on the Subject of Manufactures (December, 1791) at this link.

NASA, ESA, and the Hubble Heritage Team (STScI/AURA)

The so-called "Rose of Galaxies" (Arp 273). "It is the power of man to affect the environment which we inhabit in our species' marginal benefit," LaRouche writes, "which is the only competent standard for measurement of truth.... [A]dore progress within our Solar system, and beyond, above all else."

when it were measured on the scale of human realities. *To speak in relatively specific terms: human progress can be fairly measured, in terms of its net physical effect, per capita, as an effective increase of the net energy-flux density efficiently expressed, per capita, relevant to the environment in which human purposeful activity is effectively expressed. The notion of chemistry as such, serves currently as an excellent first approximation of the categorical, ontological species-difference of mankind from beast.* Lack of progress on that account, measures nothing as certainly as the death of economy when measured in such terms, as shown under the wretched conditions created under the alleged ministrations of the George W. Bush. Jr. and Obama Presidencies, now each approaching eight years of a still continuing pure Hell for our United States!

The popular, but thoroughly fraudulent standard, which is often substituted for that principle-of-effect, using hoaxes such as belief in sense-certainty as a standard of measurement, has a certain relevance for the effects of human behavior, but very little, in and of itself, of the relationship of the noëtic principle specific to the human mind.

The great, common error of customary beliefs, in this respect, is the presumption that sense-perception defines the reality of our species' ultimate nature, as a species. But, the truth is, that sense-perception remains merely sense-perception, always in passing, not as a conclusion, either backwards, or forwards in history, in its direction of motion. The true test, is the effect of the expressed human will on the Solar system (and beyond) as such.

This challenge, can be, and must be, assessed in terms of the effective rate of increase of the human species' immediate effect on qualitative changes in its willful effects on the living environment which we inhabit in our incarnation as human Earthlings. Yet, what are those effects? They are to be measured in the efficiently physical increase, or retrogression, of the powers of the human species over both the Earth's environment which we inhabit, our powers per-capita as contrasted with changes between rival animal and human forms of creatures, and our relative power to influence the large universe which, we, as a species,

ministration of the United States, especially that made by President George Washington's first Treasury Secretary, Alexander Hamilton.

Those opinions contrary to my own practice in an economic science, are rightly to be considered as potentially dangerous "quacks," in both intentions and effects. Presently, Franklin Roosevelt's great Glass-Steagall's achievements illustrate the point, and expose the virtually chronic insanity of any contrary, merely monetarist opinions.

However, the premises for that conclusion which I have just identified, for myself, immediately above, are not financial in any essential respect; they are exclusively "hard core-physical" in their essential nature. Money *per se* is simply a matter of masturbation, in one expression, or, another: which is exactly what Wall Street bankers might be duly doing, in lunchtime, or evening entertainments with the boys and girls, alike.

Money as such, actually "earns" absolutely nothing,

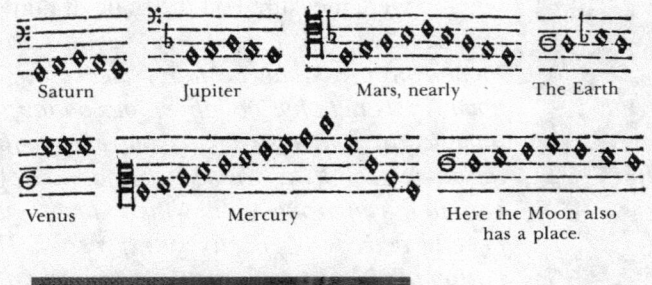

Saturn   Jupiter   Mars, nearly   The Earth

Venus   Mercury   Here the Moon also has a place.

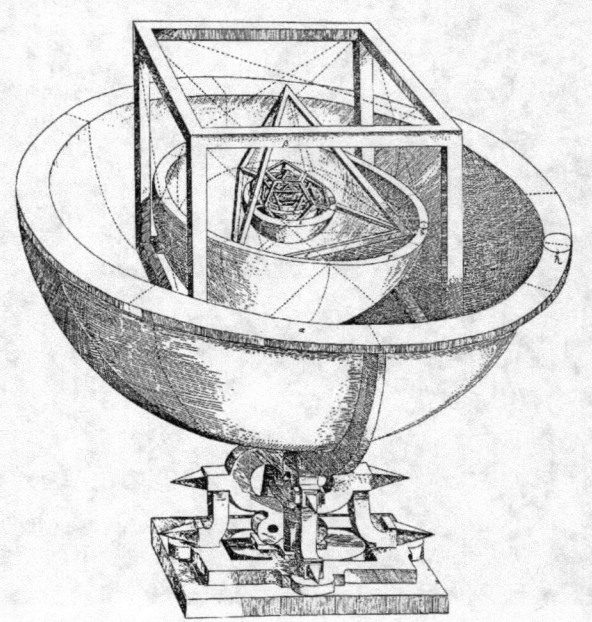

Above: Kepler's study of the harmonic relations among the planets, expressed in musical notation. Right: Kepler's geometrical model of the solar system as nested Platonic solids.

inhabit. Sense-perception, as such, has the value of some sort of masturbation performed by the human mind: i.e., "the pleasure-pain principle." Pain is useful as a warning-sign; otherwise, if considered as evidence of fact as such, it must be contained by consideration of more reliable evidence pertaining to man's evolutionary upward nature as a species as such (or, decline).

There is no accident in the evidence which we have recently tended to consider as the periodic table of chemistry and its experimental characteristics; now lately, that is undergoing, inevitably, progressive revisions within the onset of thermonuclear technologies. Yet, even then, chemistry considered as a self-evident system, has been shown to have been a wrongful presumption. It is the power of man to effect the environment which we inhabit in our species' marginal benefit, which is the only competent standard for measurement of truth. "Kill the unnecessary pain," if possible, but adore progress within our Solar system, and beyond, above all else. That, instead of the pleasure-pain standard. Protect against the pain, if you are able, but seize the opportunity of progress of man within the universe, as an integral agency-principle of the universe. Pain,

with aid of science, we can manage. Progress, as I have just now defined it, is absolutely essential, come what may.

Here lies true pleasure and pain, when sorted out, properly.

The true pleasures which man must seek, are located in the type of experiences which we might identify as what is usefully named as lawfully construed Music (Classical only), Poetry, Drama and actually physical science practiced by man on Earth and beyond, insofar as we are enabled by the development of our minds. Anything otherwise, is to be treated as garbage. All that is human, must be governed by the principle of mankind's proper devotion to a process of universal creation. That is our immortal destiny; that is, really, what we should be, as the practice of means to that end.

The principle which I have, thus, described here, must be the kernel of our motivation; and, from motivation derived from those true measures of progress of the human mind which is unique for what we may identity as the Classical artistic experience. Such are the measures, standards, and human benefits of a truly Classical art and science.

When we discover a higher quality of the future of

mankind, on Earth, as, for example, within the nearby planets and, asteroids, the mysterious overlapping of the Solar system with its galaxy, and, so on, are the truly natural expressions of human intention and resulting progress. It must become our true pleasure, to locate the notion of value in what the creative (intrinsically noëtic) powers of the human mind resonate still longer after the original discoverer were deceased, an effect then resonating as if through the heavens, as if forever. That is a clue to the true destiny and meaning of the human life. From Adam through Einstein, and beyond, that reveals the underlying, immortal experience of that which has lived to create higher principles within our universe.

II: Within the Bounds of Life

So, it must be, from generations to generations. It seems to be, at first, a mystery which could not be efficiently explained by anyone. It is, so to speak: *Just there!* Yet, nevertheless, we now know that would be a silly thing to think, or, to say. What we are (or, at least, should be) thinking, is that there must be some kind of meaning in all this. The fact that we may not actually know that meaning, in and of itself, in some explicit terms of practical considerations, does not mean that the relationship does not exist. It means, simply, that we have not yet understood this satisfactorily. Anyway, what baby had ever known, actually, *why* he, or she had been born? Whether you like the idea, or not, is pretty much an irrelevant issue in and of itself.

The issue for us, is, simply: What would be a wise course of action implicitly built into our nature, for those very reasons?

In seeking to answer such questions and related considerations, such as those, a sane riddler would examine his chances for what he might justly consider reasonably actual options for enjoying the given arrangement of affairs. Why not simply enjoy the power to discover!? It clearly seems to be what the "Boss" wishes to do; "He" leaves us no desirable option, otherwise. Thus, the composition of the Universe, however it might have been composed, seems, clearly, the "only way to go:" enjoy the ride which we call "life." After all, "the boss" was, really, always in charge. Perhaps he is a lot smarter, in his way, than we are, even in ours.

Also, there is the important fact, that the creative human powers of mankind, are the only moral expression of human existence. Creativity is the law which reigns over this universe, insofar as we know it. Do not get on the wrong side of the Creator; the results might be, foreseeably evident. The Brutish Queen's "political disease," for example, is doubtlessly a Satanic trait, as it has always been, as it is to be, therefore, a damnation of all of the cult-worshippers of the Zeusian persuasion of such as the Roman Empire, and of its avowed grandchild, the British Empire still of the present time.

So, the good grandfather, the artisan, took his grandson to view the massive construction to be comprehended by that child. The grandfather said: "I was one of those who built that!" That principle is not an expression of the grandfather's "ego;" it is the expression of his religion, his true nature, the spirit which is to be inherited by the grandson.

That is prelude; what is the substance? In other words, what does true science mean for the "small guy" representing humanity?

What Is the True Meaning of 'Vanity'?

The fool, and he is legion, says to himself, "I experienced that!" What did he actually experience? Was it not the silly pride of sense-certainties? What are our senses, after all? Are sense-certainties real? What do they actually accomplish, when we seek to explain how the Solar System actually works? Is sense-perception really ours? Or, is it our consoling fantasy? How is the evolution of our Solar System managed, in effect? Was it by merely sense-perception?

Our Sun is currently in a relatively quieted phase, and very bad for us, especially West of the Mississippi. That is, in fact, frightening. As a result, the entirety of the United States west of the Mississippi has collapsed in terms of the water of life. This had happened before; then, it went on for centuries. The water of life in the western part of our nation, is drying out, in effect; how, then, shall we live, over centuries to come? What does mere sense-perception do for us, under comparable circumstances?

Those frightening effects, and related kinds of effects, mock our foolish pride: the silly pride of saying that "I did that." Sense-perception is one of the worst whores we have seen, but, also, therefore, the most likely sexual fantasy of fools.

We, mankind on Earth, have entered a time, in which new great challenges to our species are now emerging to confront our attentions.

How mighty, in fact, is our Solar system? Is that

Solar system itself not grabbed by the more powerful fist of its galaxy? Shuttled and battered by the waves of power which the galaxy represents as in progress? What, then, of your silly pride in the virtually mere fantasy of your precious pleasure in mere sense-perception?! You are tickled: you laugh. You are hurt: you moan and curse your fate. You rule!? You, with your me-me-me chants? Your silly sense-perception, and its sillier wishes? Is sense-perception actually reality? Or, is it a kind of merely herding-device for human who must be guided in their very opinions by the whips of fate, called the bloodied thongs of mere sense-perception? Or, are they the mere whips for a blinded man, who must be bludgeoned into following the course of his destiny, by the mere blindness of sense-perception, and thus governed by more than anything else, by the lusts and whimperings of the batterings and seductions, or the lures and pains—or, of mere sense-perceptions?

Can we not, somehow, find a better guide to our proper destiny than mere sense-perception? Merely pleasure and pain? I contend, that we can find just that remedy for our existential pain; and, that that is the lesson of reality which defines the truth of human existence. That, is the true meaning of science; that, in turn, is the true meaning of the existence of our human species. That is our only true immortality as a living species.

Start with the management required for our direction of the evolution of our modest Solar system. Move asteroids! Change planets in their course! How is the Galaxy managed? What lies beyond? How long must the mere womb be our universe? What design compels us to mate? What is the intention of seeing, or hearing, of distinguishing pain from pleasure? How small-minded are our citizens generally? Sense-perception? You childish idiot!

You think that you can measure God? Design his clothing. Arrange his travel-schedules. Choose his gar-

Creative Commons/Dave Buchwald

"You came into the world a very silly, little thing, who knew not what he was, or why: all lollipops and tears, pain and pleasures." Time for the human species to grow up, to "escape the mythical characteristics of mere sense perception."

ments. A blind man could see the truth much better than you, with your pitiful pride in sense-perception. Is it not that case, that because you came into the world a very silly, little thing, who knew not what he was, or why: all lollipops and tears, pain and pleasures. What were those whips and lures all about? Why?

It is when we escape the mythical characteristics of mere sense-perception, that we begin to discover what species we really represent, rising from infancy of your mere existence as a species, to rise above, and beyond immediate experiences, to seek a higher purpose for the existence of that of which you still know almost nothing presently. To rise beyond the compulsions of infantile existence, that of mere sense-perceptions, into an education into a valid more or less of creativity respecting the universe which we inhabit.

It is time for you to change your mental diapers, voluntarily, without making a horrid mess of nearly everything in sight. Your assigned destiny is not to be that of a giant, fat and foolish baby, taken from the imaginations of the wise Rabelais, and into his insight into the meaning of Panurge! Get past the point that you must rely upon your ancient, and now very disgusting mental diapers; select a useful trade of your own making! Help fix up the universe, on your own account; then, you will mean something useful in this local universe: as Brunelleschi and Cusa had done. Then, you will be no longer stumbling infants in your very smelly, present, and dirtied, intellectual diapers.

III. The Meaning of a Human Mission

What I have written in this report, up to this present moment, can be reviewed, at this point in my report, when my preceding arguments are taken adequately into consideration.

Gustave Doré's illustration of the Sheep of Panurge jumping ship, for François Rabelais's masterwork, Gargantua and Pantagruel.

We are, in effect, possessed by a certain destiny of which we are not informed, and yet, as my remarks here so far, imply, there is an accessible view of the meaning of human life beyond merely sense-perception as such. Not some consoling fantasy, but a prescient foretaste of reality, a mere glimpse of the future of man in our universe. That means what I would otherwise mean as the passage from infancy into adult reality of members of our species. No longer should we be confined to sense-perception as taught by our kindergarten teachers, but, we must, rather, choose the inspiration of a voluntary role no longer requiring spiritual diapers. This is a role not far distant from the necessity of herding human sheep: as what the devoutly religious Rabelais must have meant by the case of "The Sheep of Panurge," and, also, the related case of the notorious woman of Paris.

It is the sheer infantilism of our fellow human creatures which must shock us into realizing, more, what we have not become, than what we think we are, which prompts the twinges of insight to the reality we, customarily childish creatures that we are, often wishfully prefer to ignore. It is a sensibility of a higher purpose, which an infantile society prefers to ignore.

The distinction to be made, on this account, resides within the notion of creativity *per se, the coming-out from the infantilism of sense-certainty, into the necessity for doing that which had been (sensually) never done, or desired before: true human creativity. No longer lured by the follies of sense-certainty's infantile delights, my own greatest sense of true pleasure is that shown by such as Cusa, Kepler, Rabelais, Shakespeare, and Schiller, and, Benjamin Franklin, Alexander Hamilton, John Quincy Adams, and the like, to make man better, actually growing up from childishness, to creative visions of a purpose for life.* To reach beyond the shackles of childishly mere customary behavior, for the benefit of the voluntary future yet to come.

Such are the greatest delights which I have been enabled yet to know.[4] The question so posed: is the meaning of the existence of human life. In the flesh, there is little to be gained, as such. But there is a higher mission, which can not be taken from us, living, or dead. To know that, is our true happiness, the passion which directs our purpose in our existing for as long as we are enabled. We are the immortal soldiers of the human soul.

---

4. It is necessary to consider the fact, that both Rabelais and Shakespeare were devoutly Christians, as was Friedrich Schiller in a very much related way. The subjects to be considered on this account, are the faults and higher intentions of mankind within the ordering of the true universe, not necessarily the merely sense-perceptual one. The passage from the shackles of sense-perception, to the freedom of the human spirit which lies beyond, defines the true human intellect and embedded purpose of the post-larval phase of the existence of the adult, and of the truly immortal human soul. The greatest and best ambition is to be such a truly free human soul.

All of the greatest scientists and poets have lived for that purpose, above all others. For us, it must be our only truest ambition. We are the real, truly immortal scientists of the human soul: it is the properly adopted meaning of our existence, to have lived and acted so. In that way, we shall never die: we are built into the existence of our universe, as our greatest scientists have demonstrated this: even when long deceased, thus, as the greatest of our scientists and poets have done before. We are not the chattel of Zeus, and never will be: thus, the martyrs have cheated the devil himself, and will enjoy a truly sweet revenge against evil *per se.* All of our greatest scientists and poets have done the same: we make the future; that is our profession; that is our strategy, of which, we are assured, that nothing can prevent. The planets may be destroyed, solar systems and the like, may pass, but we are ever there, jerking the devil's tail as if by invisible hands, wherever, and whatever we may become beyond. We are joined together in this mission, throughout it all, forever. That is the meaning of a human life having been lived.

EDITORIAL

What Everyone Is Pretending Not to Notice

June 22—It is widely expected that Presidents Trump and Putin will meet in person for the first time on the sidelines of the July 7-8 Group of 20 (G20) summit in Hamburg. This meeting has the potential to be a world-changing event. As we have reported, Russian Senator Alexander Pushkov said on June 20 that this meeting will be the highlight of the G20 summit if it takes place. "A lot will depend on this meeting," he said, and "that is why it is so highly anticipated everywhere—from Tallin to Lisbon, from Beijing to Cairo." Yes, it's critically important—but yet no one is talking about it! It's "hiding in plain view," as Lyndon LaRouche has frequently cited a notion found in Edgar Allan Poe's story of "The Purloined Letter."

Our adversaries of the British imperial faction are saying absolutely nothing about this fast approaching Trump-Putin summit, because they are terribly frightened of what may happen there. After all, why else have the neocons and neoliberals spent so many months lying their heads off that President Trump and his associates are somehow Russian agents? Now this imminent summit is so important that they refuse even to mention it!

Instead, they have been moving in obvious ways to try to get the Trump-Putin meeting cancelled—or, if they can't get it cancelled, to try to ensure that it is ruined, and that it becomes totally hostile, so that no positive personal relationship can develop.

It was for this reason that a crazy Russia sanctions bill was rammed through the Senate by a lopsided 98-2 majority just one week ago today—and then misreported as "Trump sanctions" by the lying British-run media—even though the Trump Administration opposes it and is trying to stop it before it can become law. It was for this reason that U.S. forces shot down a Syrian jet on June 18, forcing the Russians to again terminate

the hotline through which U.S. and Russian forces had deconflicted their operations in Syria. It was for this reason that Steve Mnuchin's U.S. Treasury Department imposed sanctions on 38 Russian and Ukrainian firms and individuals on June 20, forcing Russia to cancel a planned meeting between Deputy Foreign Minister Ryabkov and U.S. Under Secretary of State Thomas Shannon. And whose F-16 was it that buzzed the jet of Russian Defense Minister Shoigu just yesterday?

And what worse treasonous act will these people commit tomorrow, in their hysteria over the prospect of better relations between the United States and Russia?

These sinister forces have refused to recognize the Constitutional election decision of the American people since day one, and they still refuse. Those of us who support the President and the Constitution must come forth to crush the forces of treason, and to support the President to achieve his objectives by joining the United States with Russia and China in the New Silk Road and recreating American infrastructure through massive Federal credit—and in partnership with China, through Lyndon LaRouche's Four New Laws of June 2014. And tomorrow may be too late.

Further indication of the British-loving layer's hysteria at the prospect of a linking-up of Putin with Trump, can be found in German Finance Minister Wolfgang Schäuble's remarks on June 20, upon receiving the Henry Kissinger Prize: "I doubt whether the United States truly believes that the world order would be equally sound if China or Russia were to fill the gaps left by the United States, and if China and Russia were simply given a free hand to dominate the spheres of influence that they have defined for themselves. That would be the end of our liberal world order."

He's lying, and he knows he's lying—but can't you feel the hysteria behind his lying?